LIKE MAGIC

A Series of Computerized Cases For Managerial and Cost Accounting

THIRD EDITION

MICHAEL A. KOLE
Rider University

Prentice Hall
Upper Saddle River, New Jersey 07458

Acquisitions editor: *Deborah Emry*
Associate editor: *Lori Cardillo Cerreto*
Project editor: *Theresa Festa*
Manufacturers: *Quebecor Printing Group*

© 1999 by Prentice Hall, Inc.
Upper Saddle River, New Jersey 07458

All rights reserved. No part of this book may be reproduced, in any form or by any means, without permission in writing from the publisher.

Printed in the United States of America

10 9 8 7 6 5 4 3

ISBN 0-13-012895-3

PRENTICE-HALL INTERNATIONAL (UK) LIMITED, LONDON
PRENTICE-HALL OF AUSTRALIA PTY. LIMITED, SYDNEY
PRENTICE-HALL CANADA INC., TORONTO
PRENTICE-HALL HISPANOAMERICANA, S.A., MEXICO
PRENTICE-HALL OF INDIA PRIVATE LIMITED, NEW DELHI
PRENTICE-HALL OF JAPAN, INC., TOKYO
PEARSON EDUCATION ASIA PTE. LTD., SINGAPORE
EDITORA PRENTICE-HALL DO BRASIL, LTDA., RIO DE JANEIRO

TO   JOY, LARRY, ALI, and LEIGH

Michael A. Kole is Associate Professor of Accounting at Rider University. He received his B.Mgt.Eng. degree from Rensselaer Polytechnic Institute and his Ph.D. degree from the University of Massachusetts.

Professor Kole has provided consultation to numerous organizations on management accounting and information technology. He has developed and delivered professional workshops on the use of electronic spreadsheets and computer databases for accounting and investment to audiences in a number of sectors of our society. Kole has numerous publications and presentations in accounting and information systems. He has contributed text and cases to books in cost accounting and management.

LIKE MAGIC

A SERIES OF COMPUTER CASES

FOR MANAGEMENT and COST ACCOUNTING

CONTENTS

Preface viii

1	**Case Narrative and Introduction to the Assignments** 1	
A	Company Background 1	
B	Introduction to the Assignments 1	

2	**Cost-Volume-Profit Relationships** 3	
A	Break-even Analysis and Graphing 3	
B	What If? Planning Under Varying Assumptions 6	

3	**Cost Estimation** 9	
A	The Visual-Fit and High-Low Methods 9	
B	Linear Regression 12	

4 **Cost Management Systems** 19
A Income Statement – Absorption Approach 19
B Income Statement – Contribution Approach, Variable and Fixed Costs per Unit, and International Aspects of Labor Cost Content 22

5 **Relevant Costs for Decision Making** 26
A Special Sales Orders 26
B Cost-plus Pricing and Special Orders 28
C Optimal Use of Limited Resources 30

6 **Relevant Costs for Make or Buy Decision Making** 33

7 **Budgeting** 38
A Operating Budget 38
B Cash Budget 40
C A Budgeted Balance Sheet 43

8	**Flexible Budgets and Variance Analysis** 48	
A	Master and Flexible Budget Variances 48	
B	Price and Usage Variances 50	
9	**Control in Decentralized Organizations** 53	
A	Performance Measures 53	
B	Transfer Pricing 56	
10	**Capital Budgeting** 59	
A	Discounted Cash Flow and Sensitivity Analysis 59	
B	Effects of Income Taxes on Capital Budgeting 63	
11	**Allocation of Service Department Costs** 67	
A	The Direct Method 67	
B	The Step Method 69	
12	**Activity-Based Costing** 72	
13	**Overhead Application** 76	
A	Applying Factory Overhead 76	
B	Accounting at the End of the Year 78	
14	**Process-Costing Systems** 82	
A	The Initial Department 82	
B	A Subsequent Department 85	
C	Standard Costs in Process Costing 87	
15	**The Statement of Cash Flows** 93	
A	The Direct Method 93	
B	The Indirect Method 96	
C	Additional Cash Flows 98	
16	**Analysis of Financial Statements** 102	
A	Component Percentages and Year-to-Year Changes 102	
B	Ratio Analysis 105	

APPENDIX: Excel – Enhancing Your Skills 109

PREFACE

<u>Like Magic Company - A Series of Computer Cases for Management and Cost Accounting</u> is designed to help people learn management and cost accounting in a computer-based environment. This book will also assist in learning Microsoft ™ Excel spreadsheet software. Its aim is proficiency in using an accounting database and an electronic spreadsheet for management planning, control, and decision making. Helpful ways of using Excel are suggested throughout the chapters and in the appendix to improve efficiency and effectiveness.

This book is intended to accompany texts presenting theory. The book can also be used in seminars and by people working independently to expand their knowledge of electronic spreadsheet use in a management accounting context.

The chapter sequence and topical coverage follow *Introduction to Management Accounting, Eleventh Edition* by Horngren, Sundem and Stratton. The approach taken and report formats in this book make it an effective supplement to many texts.

Features

This book contains many features to enhance student learning, minimize instructors' time, make the decision situations realistic, and provide flexibility of assignments. The following are some of its key features:

1. A student computer disk is included with the book. The disk contains report formats in template form for each chapter. Because the report formats are similar to those used in many textbooks, students concentrate on creating correct relationships and entering formulas in appropriate locations, following the way the material was learned. These standard report formats make solution presentation by students and/or instructors much clearer and easier to understand. Grading is also speeded up.

2. Recalculations for differing time periods or data sets are often required and can be done very rapidly. Questions are stated which use the results to reinforce the theory being learned.

3. Graphs of results are supplements to some assignments and serve to provide demonstrations of the important issues.

4. Tables with all necessary input data are presented on the student disk to minimize time and errors in data entry.

5. All chapters are based upon one firm with internally consistent data. This is beneficial for classroom discussions and multi-chapter assignments such as end of the term projects.

6. Chapters can be assigned in any sequence. The data for each chapter is presented with the computer file and narrative for the chapter.

7. The material simulates building models and doing analysis in a business-like setting using a personal computer and Microsoft Excel.

8. The book presumes basic computer and spreadsheet experience using Excel. Helpful ways of using Excel are suggested throughout the chapters and in the appendix to improve efficiency and effectiveness.

9. The cases and the supplement have helped many people learn management and cost accounting, and expand their ability to use electronic spreadsheets.

To the Instructor

Microsoft Excel is now used for all of the spreadsheets in this third edition. The chapters and appendix contain suggestions to improve efficiency in using Excel. All files have been created in Excel 5.0/95.

The third edition of Like Magic improves on the cases presented in the second edition and corrects some minor problems. A new chapter, 13, has been added on activity costing. Moderate changes have been made to report formats and/or data in Chapters 2 on cost-volume-profit and 3 on cost estimation. A contribution margin income statement and the use (or not) of a JIT system have been added to Chapter 4 on cost systems, while the supporting schedules for the absorption income statement have been eliminated. The topic on relevant costs for decision making has been expanded and separated into two chapters: Chapter 5 covers marketing decisions, and 6 covers production decisions. A section on master and flexible budget variance analysis has been added to Chapter 8 on variances. Improvements in report formats and some data changes have been made to the other chapters.

The cases have been designed to minimize your time and allow you to concentrate on teaching accounting. Students must clearly understand the concepts and relationships to enter the formulas to complete each assignment. Reinforcement occurs from recalculation, graphing, and answering questions that are part of each chapter. No macros are included. Students must use Excel to solve and output all solutions. The material and solutions lend themselves to classroom discussions. Students can and have done the assignments completely on their own. You don't have to teach spreadsheets and computer use, or make up assignments. The solutions disk gives you the results and the formulas in the same standard report formats the students are using. These standard report solutions are very beneficial for classroom presentation by you or your students. Time to correct student results can be minimized by using the solution and student disks.

I usually assign students to work in teams of 2-4 people. This approach encourages students to help each other and usually makes the work more interesting. To insure that all students are doing the work, I either have them present the solutions or call on students. Sometimes I put questions on exams based upon the solutions in the book.

An approach that I have used for my accounting information systems course is to require Chapters 4 on cost systems, 12 on cash flows, and 13 on dealing with financial statements and their analysis. A project is then assigned with a choice from the following requirements: 1) Use goal setting and create budgeted statements for the following year. 2) Obtain, input and analyze comparable data for real organizations. 3) Prepare a written analysis of the benefits and detriments of using spreadsheets for financial statement creation and presentation.

A solution disk is available.

Chapter Content

Each chapter contains:

1. Learning objectives
2. A narrative which describes the business situation
3. Requirements to be completed
4. Computer information on file names
5. Printed worksheets containing the data and templates that will be seen on the computer screen
6. Check figures

Chapters can be selected in any sequence. Most chapters contain parts A and B, and some a part C. Part A is always easier and uses more elementary concepts. Part A can always be assigned without requiring B or C. The few chapters where part B can be done without first doing part A are noted at the start of the chapter.

The time to complete each requirement will vary, often based upon the user's facility with Excel. If solution time is a concern, eliminating some requirements can shorten many assignments.

Using Like Magic Company with a Text

These computer cases can be easily used as a supplement to a text in managerial or cost accounting. The organization of the chapters, approach to the subject, report formats and terminology have been designed to follow Introduction to Management Accounting, Eleventh Edition by Horngren, Sundem and Stratton. The material in these cases is consistent with many chapters in Accounting, Fourth Edition by Horngren, Harrison and Bamber, and Cost Accounting Ninth Edition by Horngren, Foster and Datar.

Like Magic Company builds on the emphasis in those books. The approach taken stimulates thinking and encourages curiosity. Students use the spreadsheets and company data to provide information and recommended decisions for managerial planning, control and decision making.

The following table cross-references the chapters in Like Magic Company with the three aforesaid books.

CHAPTER CROSS REFERENCE

Like Magic	Horngren/ Sundem/ Stratton	Horngren/ Harrison/ Bamber	Horngren/ Foster/ Datar
2	2	22	3
3	3		10
4	4	19	4,5
5	5	26	11,12
6	6	26	11
7	7	26	6
8	8	24	7,8
9	10		25,26
10	11	26	22,23
11	12	23	13,14
12	12	25	4
13	13	20	5
14	14	21	17
15	17	17	
16	18	18	

To the Student - Getting Started

You are expected to have a basic knowledge of Microsoft Excel spreadsheet software to use this book. You will become more proficient at Excel if you share questions and answers with a friend who is learning at the same time.

Most students will begin to learn in the personal computer laboratory of their school. You only need the disk contained in the back of this book. Keeping two disks is a great idea for backup protection in case problems result with the data on one of the disks. If you use two disks, periodically copy the files on the Like Magic disk onto the second disk.

To begin using the computer, take this manual and your disk to the computer lab. Ask to use a personal computer that contains Microsoft Excel. If you have never worked in the lab, ask for help to begin. If you are using your own computer, you will need a copy of Excel as well as the disk contained in this book.

Spreadsheet Software

Microsoft Excel 5.0/95 is used in this book. Most spreadsheet software that can import Excel files can be used to do the assignments in this book.

LIKE MAGIC COMPANY

Chapter 1: Case Narrative and Introduction to the Assignments

A. Company Background

Four years ago Tom Turner developed a new type of cream to improve skin appearance. After a few weeks of tests, his wife Tracy and her friends declared that the cream worked like magic. Keeping the formula a closely guarded secret, Tracy and Tom Turner started the Like Magic Company to manufacture this new type of skin cream.

Tom and Tracy gave up their jobs and put all of their financial assets into the business. Tom was responsible for development and manufacturing, while Tracy took charge of marketing and finance. Tom converted their garage into a production and development center. The family room became the storage, packing and shipping area. Tracy ran the sales from the kitchen.

Sales started with friends and grew by word of mouth. Tracy convinced a few local retailers to carry Like Magic. As sales increased, products, boxes, papers, etc. took over their house. Every room became work space. Expansion was necessary, so they took out a second mortgage on their house, rented space and began adding staff. Business kept growing and so did the need for more people, inventory, equipment, and space.

As cash started to run short, Tom and Tracy turned to Rodney Rukeyser and his investment group for additional financing. Like Magic received additional capital in exchange for expanded ownership and the agreement to sell shares in the company to the public the following year.

Over the past four years, Like Magic has achieved a considerable measure of success. Sales have increased very nicely and Like Magic is an important segment of a growing market. Shares of their stock are owned by the public and actively traded. The market price of their stock is widely reported by the financial press.

Like Magic is planning on significant expansion for next year. They are negotiating to purchase a small company producing another skin care cream. They are also in discussion to buy the rights to produce another cream from a European manufacturer. Like Magic is planning to sell their cream internationally, with Canada the likely first target, then Mexico, Europe and Asia. All of this will require purchase of new buildings and equipment, which in turn will necessitate new financing.

B. Introduction to the Assignments

You have just been hired as controller of Like Magic. The accounting staff has entered relevant information into several new Excel spreadsheets that were developed by the company's consultant. Like Magic's officers want you to provide financial information and analysis for the past year and the coming year. They would like to see data, discussion, and recommendations evaluating their performance, helping to improve financial control, and supporting decisions on future directions for the company.

You will be guided in doing your analysis through the assignments presented in the chapters. Each chapter is independent of the others and can be selected in any order.

A separate spreadsheet is provided for each chapter. Each chapter lists the name of the file to be used for that assignment. These spreadsheets provide all of the data that you will need and give you the report layouts that you will complete. These spreadsheets were created in Excel and have been saved in files on the disk that came with this book. **Files are saved in Excel 5.0/95 file format.** This means you can work in Excel 97, Excel 95 or Excel version 5.0.

How to Start

First read the company background in this chapter. Next, read the assigned chapter and review the worksheet at the end as you are reading the requirements for that chapter. Place checkmarks on the worksheet next to a few items that need to be completed. Using a calculator, compute some of the figures and write them on the worksheet. For example, in Chapter 2 the first requirement is to compute the per unit total variable cost and contribution margin. Compute these figures and write them on the worksheet. Compare your contribution margin per unit with the given check figure at the end of the chapter.

Now go to the computer and start Excel. (If you've never used Excel before, work with a partner or get someone to help you.) From the menu at the top of the screen select **File**, **Open**, look in **Floppy (A:)**. Then select the name of the file that is specified in the chapter to open and open it. Follow the requirements to complete the assignment.

Remember to periodically save your work, but save it under a new file name so the original file data is not changed. Suggested file names for saving are given in each chapter. Also remember to insert your name in the print header line as describe below.

Print Header – Entering Your Name

A print header line has been created so it prints on each page of every chapter. The following commands will enable you to insert your name in the print header line so your name prints on each page.

- Select **File** from the menu at the top of the screen.
- Select **Page Setup** from the drop-down menu.
- Select **Header/Footer** from the drop-down menu.
- Select **Customer Header** from the box in the middle of the screen.
- Position the pointer in the **Right section** and click the mouse.
- Enter **"Your Name"**.
- Select **OK** from the box on the right.
- Select **OK** from the box at the bottom.
- Save the file.

LIKE MAGIC COMPANY

Chapter 2. Cost-Volume-Profit Relationships

A: Break-even Analysis and Graphing

A. LEARNING OBJECTIVES

1. Gain understanding of variable costing and the contribution margin.
2. Learn the value of using variable cost and contribution margin percentages of sales.
3. Learn how to compute the break-even point in units and dollars
4. Prepare a cost-volume-profit graph from an electronic spreadsheet.

B. NARRATIVE

Tom Turner, Like Magic's President, has just called an executive committee meeting to start planning for the coming year. A few quick phone calls reveal that Fawn Fonda, Vice President of Marketing, plans to come to the meeting with a schedule of various selling price and volume combinations. Anthony Iococca, Vice President of Manufacturing, will have some requests for expansion of plant and equipment. Fidel Fernandez, Director of Purchasing, will try to find some cheaper sources of supply for materials and other production costs, or at least what the going market prices will be next year. Finally, Willy Wang, Director of Research and Development, isn't sure that he will have the cost estimates on the planned new products.

You decide to develop a spreadsheet model on your personal computer including a contribution margin analysis, break-even point calculations, and a cost-volume-profit graph. With the spreadsheet model and the computer in the meeting, you will be able to answer many "what if" questions and help the executive committee narrow down its choices of actions for next year. Hopefully, this approach will reduce the length of the meeting and reduce the number of follow-up meetings.

C. REQUIREMENTS

1. Review Worksheet 2 at the end of this chapter. The selling price, variable costs and fixed expenses were copied from the books and plans of Like Magic. They are average values for the past year. Compute some of the required figures before you go to the computer.

2. Use Excel to open the file **CVP**.

3. The first section presents Like Magic's selling price and variable costs for each unit. Using this data, compute the **per unit total variable cost** in cell **C9**, and **per unit contribution margin**, **C10**. Format to two decimal places.

4. Compute the **total yearly fixed expenses** in cell **C16**, from the three figures presented for the yearly fixed expenses.

5. The column next to the per unit figures should be used to calculate each per unit figure as a percentage of the selling price. Use these **cells, D4-D10**, to compute the **selling price, each variable cost, the total variable cost and contribution margin** as a percentage of the selling price and format with one decimal place. Example: for the percentage of sales corresponding to the selling price, in cell D4, the formula is C4/C4, or 32/32, which the computer will calculate and display as 100%. (You can save time by using the **Copy** command in Excel, especially if you copy using an absolute reference. Since each percentage will be calculated by dividing each per unit figure by the selling price, the denominator should be an absolute reference in the formula in the first cell before copying to other cells. In cell D4 the formula would be C4/$C$4. Absolute references are specified by putting a $ sign in front of the row and column references in a formula. Then if the formula in cell D4 is copied to cells D5-D10, the correct formulas, and therefore results, will appear.)

6. Develop and insert the formulas (equations) for **break-even sales in units** in **cell C18** and for **break-even sales in dollars** in **cell C19**. See the text under the Equation Method for the formulas.

7. Complete the **Cost-Volume-Profit Relationship Table, B23-J27**. This is done by entering formulas to compute the total sales dollars, expenses and net income in each column beneath the given number of units sold. (You can save time by using the **Copy** command with absolute references just as shown in #5 above.)

8. Create an **XY Cost-Volume-Profit Graph** by plotting lines for the sales dollars and total expenses using Excel and the data in the Cost-Volume-Profit Relationship Table. Put titles on the graphs using the spreadsheet. See the appendix for creating a chart using Excel, for help with creating the graph.

9. Print the entire spreadsheet and the graph you created. Before the report is printed, insert your name into the Print Header Line. (See Print Header Line in Chapter 1.)

10. Save your results in the file **CVPR**.

11. Compare the numerical calculation of the break-even point with the point on the two graphs. Do the break-even points agree? Indicate on the graph the areas for net loss and net profit. Explain why the areas of net profit and net loss grow wider as the distance from the break-even point increases.

D. COMPUTER INFORMATION

1. Name of the file to be retrieved: **CVP**
2. Name of the file to save results: **CVPR**
3. Cell locations: **A1-J27**

See the appendix for computer information on copying, graphing and setting up a print header.

E.   WORKSHEET 2: Cost-Volume-Profit Analysis

F.   CHECK FIGURES

	Figures	Cell Location
Contribution margin per unit	$ 14.05	C10
Break-even sales: units	$ 800	C18
Net income at 200 units sold	$ (8,435)	C27

LIKE MAGIC COMPANY

Chapter 2-B: What If? Planning Under Varying Assumptions

A. LEARNING OBJECTIVES

1. Learn how changes in selling prices, volumes, variable costs and fixed expenses affect operating income, contribution margins and break-even points using "What if" scenarios.
2. Demonstrate the speed and flexibility of electronic spreadsheets to present data in numerical form under varying planning assumptions.
3. Use a spreadsheet to demonstrate how changes in cost structure affect operating leverage.

B. NARRATIVE

Everyone liked the spreadsheet analysis that you did. Executive Vice President Tracy Turner wants to start planning for next year. She turns to you and wants to estimate how much Like Magic can earn next year. Tracy wants the first projection to keep the selling price at the average of last year, $32.00. Fawn Fonda says at that price we should be able to sell 1,375,000 units. The staff supplies their best estimates of costs at that volume. These figures are given in the first column in the Table of Estimated Data in Worksheet 2.

Tom Turner wants to see projected income when the selling price is lowered to $30.00 and raised to $35.00. Fawn wants to maintain the selling price at $32.00 and keep volume high by spending more on sales incentives. Tony Iococca proposes manufacturing automation changes that would reduce total direct labor costs requiring fewer people with higher skills. Tony's proposal would increase fixed manufacturing overhead at a volume of 1,375,000 units. Fidel Fernandez says that with the new equipment he can switch suppliers for savings in indirect production costs. As a result of the discussion, five more sets of projections are developed and shown in the Table of Estimated Data in Worksheet 2.

You suggest that the staff consider some of the non-quantitative issues of these alternatives while you enter the data and run the projections through the electronic spreadsheet.

C. REQUIREMENTS

1. Retrieve or continue working with file **CVPR**.

2. Insert formulas to calculate the **contribution margin per unit** and the **contribution margin ratio** for the past year in **cells C36 and C37**. Next, calculate the contribution margin per unit and the contribution margin ratio for the five columns in the Table of Estimated Data for Planning. You can use the Copy command to copy the two formulas in **cells C36-C37** to **cells D36-H37**.

3. Total the **fixed expenses** for the past year and the Table of Estimated Data for Planning, **cell C42-H42**.

4. Insert the formula for **break-even sales in $** into **cell C44**. (This is the same formula you developed in part A.) Develop the formula for **target net income** and enter it into cell **C45**. (See the text for the formula.) Calculate the break-even sales and the target net income for the five columns in the Table of Estimated Data for Planning. You can use the Copy command to copy the two formulas in **cells C44-C45** to **cells D44-H45.**

5. Look at the information in rows 47-51. Compare Like Magic's cost structure before automation, as given in Worksheet 2 for the past year, with what it would be after automation considering the changes indicated. As shown, automation would decrease variable labor costs per unit by $6, and increase fixed manufacturing expenses by $8,000,000. Enter the words **Higher** and **Lower** in **cells B51** and **D51** to indicate whether **operating leverage** would be higher or lower before or after automation.

6. Print the entire spreadsheet.

7. Save your results in the file **CVPR**.

8. Compare and comment on the target net income and break-even sales under each set of projections. Which projection should Like Magic set as its target? Why?

OPTIONAL REQUIREMENTS

Suggest additional "what if" data estimates. Provide logical reasons for your estimates. Add your estimates to the worksheet and print the results.

D. COMPUTER INFORMATION

1. Name of the file to be retrieved: **CVPR**
2. Name of the file to save results: **CVPR**
3. Cell locations: **A1-J51**

Worksheet 2   Like Magic Company

COST-VOLUME-PROFIT ANALYSIS

Like Magic Company	Per Unit	Percentage of Sales
Selling price	$ 32.00	
Material cost	6.00	
Labor cost	8.00	
Other production cost	1.95	
Sales incentives cost	2.00	
Total variable cost		
Contribution margin		
Yearly fixed expenses		
Manufacturing	$ 4,324	
Marketing	5,116	
Administrative	1,805	
Total fixed expenses		
Break-even sales: units	=	
Break-even sales: $	=	

Cost-Volume-Profit Table for Graphing

Units sold	0	200	400	600	800	1,000	1,200	1,400	1,600
Sales $									
Variable expenses									
Fixed expenses									
Total expenses									
Net income $									

Table of Estimated Data for Planning

		Past Year					
Sales in units		1100	1375	1540	1210	1540	1375
Selling price	per unit	$ 32.00	32.00	30.00	34.00	32.00	32.00
Material cost	" "	6.00	6.30	6.30	6.30	6.30	6.30
Labor cost	" "	8.00	8.40	8.40	8.40	8.40	4.00
Other production cost	" "	1.95	2.05	2.05	2.05	2.05	1.30
Sales incentives cost	" "	2.00	2.10	2.10	2.10	3.00	2.10
Contribution margin	" "						
Contribution margin ratio (%)							
Yearly fixed expenses							
Manufacturing		$ 4,324	4,500	4,500	4,500	4,500	11,000
Marketing		5,116	6,200	6,200	6,200	6,200	6,200
Administrative		1,805	2,100	2,100	2,100	2,100	2,100
Total fixed expenses							
Break-even sales in $							
Target net income							

	Before Automation	After Automation	
Cost Structure	As given above	$ (6)	decrease in variable labor costs per unit
		$ 8,000	increase in fixed manufacturing expenses
Operating Leverage -->			

LIKE MAGIC COMPANY

Chapter 3: Cost Estimation

A: The Visual-Fit and High-Low Methods

A. LEARNING OBJECTIVES

1. Gain understanding of the issues and assumptions involved in estimating cost functions.
2. Learn alternative methods for estimating costs.
3. Analyze a scatter graph from a set of data.
4. Demonstrate how to visually fit a line through cost points on a scatter diagram.
5. Learn how to analyze a mixed cost by the two-point (high-low) method.

B. NARRATIVE

As the year comes to an end, top management of Like Magic is developing plans for next year. Anthony Iococca, Vice President of Manufacturing, knows that sound cost estimation is important in financial planning decisions. He wants your help in developing a cost estimating function for overhead costs. You recommend selecting the variable that is the best predictor of overhead costs as the base in their formula for applying overhead. The best predictor should be the independent variable that best explains and is most closely correlated to fluctuations in overhead costs. Anthony chose three possible independent variables for the analysis. You gather data for each month in the last two years for analysis. Anthony estimated next year's total figures for the three variables.

The relationship between each of the three variables and overhead costs will be examined. By inspecting a plot of overhead costs against each independent variable, you can observe these relationships. For each plot or scatter graph you will visually fit a line through the points. This will help you decide whether overhead costs can be estimated by a linear function of that variable. To confirm your observation use the simplified two-point (high-low) approach on an electronic spreadsheet to establish a linear cost estimation function. Next, use the computer to plot the lines connecting the two points on each scatter graph. (In part B of this assignment each cost estimation relationship will be analyzed using the regression function in Excel.) The conclusion of your analysis should be a recommendation of which independent variable to select for use in the overhead cost formula for Like Magic.

C. REQUIREMENTS

1. Review Worksheet 3. Note the actual data by month for the dependent variable overhead expense and the three independent variables: production units, labor hours and machine hours. In Assignment 3-A you will use the spreadsheet to calculate the "variable" and "fixed" portions of the formula for estimating the mixed overhead cost using the high-low method. Next, you will estimate next year's overhead expenses using the high-low method for the three variables. Then you will calculate estimates of what the overhead

expenses would have been for the last 24 months if Like Magic had used the high-low method. You will use these monthly high-low estimates to plot a cost estimation line. (The calculations, data and graphs for the regression will be completed as part of assignment 3-B.)

2. Turn to the printed graphs of overhead costs and independent variables. Visually fit and draw a line through the points on each graph. Does there appear to be approximate linear relationships between overhead costs and each of the three variables? If any of the relationships are not approximately linear, what should you recommend to Like Magic?

3. Use Excel to retrieve the file **ESTIMATE**.

4. Use the two-point approach to develop formulas for estimating overhead expense based upon actual production units. Select the high and low values of actual production units as the points for your computation.

a. Calculate the "variable" portion by inserting the correct formula in **cell D31**. Format to two decimals. (See the text for the formula.)

b. Calculate the "fixed" portion in **cell D32**. Format to one decimal.

c. Use the portions of the mixed cost developed in a and b above and the projection for next year's production units in cell C33 to calculate next year's estimated overhead expense in **cell D33**. (Remember the fixed portion in D32 is a monthly amount.)

5. Use the figures developed in #4 to estimate the overhead expenses Like Magic would have calculated for each of the last 24 months. Develop estimated overhead values by creating formulas in **cells D6-D29**. Use the actual production units for each month and the figures you computed for the variable and fixed portions of overhead, cells D31-D32.

6. Use Excel to plot a line through the points you developed in #5 above using the high-low approach.

a. Use the mouse to select the chart sheet named **Chart-Prod. Units**, at the bottom of the screen, in the current file **ESTIMATE**. Entering the following commands will cause a graph like the printed worksheet to appear on the screen.

b. Make the estimated overhead values you created for each of the 24 months (# 5 above) a second series or range. The following discussion based upon Excel 97 should help you with this graphing task. (If you are using Excel 5.0/95 the commands may be a little different.)

- Select **Chart** from the menu bar at the top of the screen.
- Select **Source Data** from the menu that drops down.
- Select **Series** from the choices that appear above the chart.
- Select **Add** from the choices below the chart.
- Enter **High-Low** in the space next to "Name."
- Enter **=Estimate!$C$6:$C$29** in the space next to "X Value."

10

- Enter **=Estimate!$D$6:$D$29** in the space next to "Y Value."
- Select **OK**.
- The chart will display a plot of points of the estimated overhead costs based upon your high-low formula.
- Select **Chart** again from the top of the screen.
- Select **Add Trendline** from the menu that drops down.
- Select **High-Low** from the box at the bottom left titled "Based on series."
- Select **OK**.
- The chart will display a straight line drawn through the points formed from your high-low formula.

c. View the graph you have created and make any additional changes that you desire. Both a line and symbols appear for the high-low series (range). Note that the line that appears on the graph goes through the two points you used in your formula.

7. Repeat steps 4-6 above using labor hours as the independent variable. The results from step 4 will go into **cells G31-G33**, and step 5 into **cells G6-G29**. Select the chart sheet named **Chart-Labor Hrs.** Change the X range to the Labor hours figures.

8. Repeat steps 4-6 above using machine hours as the independent variable. The results from step 4 will go into **cells J31-J33**, and step 5 into **cells J6-J29**. Select the chart sheet named **Chart-Machine Hrs.** Change the X range to the Machine hours figures.

9. Save your results in the file **ESTIMATR**.

10. If you are not going to do assignment 3-B, print your results. Assignment 3-B has you print graphs with lines for both the high-low and linear regression estimates on the same graphs. Before printing, insert your name into the Print Header Line. (See Print Header Line in Chapter 1.)

D. COMPUTER INFORMATION

1. Name of the file to be retrieved: **ESTIMATE**
2. Name of the file to save results: **ESTIMATR**
3. Cell location for results: **D9-D36, G9-G36, J9-J36**

See the appendix section on Graphing Data for information on using Excel for graphing.

E. WORKSHEET 3: Analysis of Cost Behavior and Cost Estimation

Graphs of Overhead Costs vs. Production Units, Labor Hours, and Machine Hours

CHECK FIGURES

	Figures	Cell Location
Prod. Units - Variable Portion	2.33	D31
Machine Hours – Next year estimate	7741	J33
Jan. Estimated Overhead-Prod.Units	383	D6

LIKE MAGIC COMPANY

Chapter 3-B: Linear Regression

A. LEARNING OBJECTIVES

1. Learn how to analyze a mixed cost using the linear regression function in an electronic spreadsheet.
2. Demonstrate how to evaluate different cost estimation functions of the same cost objective.

B. NARRATIVE

You have become familiar with the data for estimating overhead costs. Visual examination and a simple two-point method have provided some insight into the relationships between three independent variables and the behavior of overhead costs. However, you are not confident enough to recommend which variable Like Magic should select for their cost estimation equation.

Regression analysis uses a statistical model to determine the best available straight-line estimate of the cost behavior function. The model also provides information on the goodness of fit of the line through the data points. Regression analysis should add support for your recommendation.

You decide to use ordinary least squares to create linear regression lines for each of the three independent variables. Excel includes a regression command as one of its tools. This command will provide a coefficient of determination or R^2 measuring the goodness of fit for each regression relationship. You will use the goodness of fit to provide reassurance to management that they should have a reasonable degree of faith in the cost estimating function that you will recommend for use.

C. REQUIREMENTS

1. Retrieve or continue working with file **ESTIMATR**.

2. Use linear regression to calculate next year's estimated overhead expenses based upon production units. All 24 months of data should be included in the computation of the regression. The following Excel 97 commands will compute the regression. (If you are using Excel 5.0/95 the commands may be a little different.)

a. Select **Tools** from the menu bar at the top of the screen. If "Data Analysis" appears at the bottom of the drop-down menu skip b and go to c, if it does not appear go to b.

b. From the drop-down menu select **Add-Ins**, select **Analysis Tool Pak**, and select **Tools** from the menu bar at the top of the screen.

c. Select **Data Analysis**

- Scroll down the choices in the box on the screen until **Regression** appears.
- Select **Regression.**
- Enter the input range for Y: **B6:B29**, the data range of actual overhead expenses.
- Enter the input range for X: **C6:C29**, the data range of actual production units.
- Click in the circle in front of the words "Output Range."
- Enter the output range: **M1:U18**, an unused area in the spreadsheet.
- Press the "Enter" key and Excel will calculate the regression displaying the results in **M1:U18**.

d. Copy the Regression Output to the cells under Regression for Production Units as follows:
- The "Coefficient of the X Variable 1" in cell N18, is copied to the Variable Portion **E31**. Format to two decimals.
- The "Coefficient of the Intercept" in cell N17, is copied to the Fixed Portion **E32**. Format to one decimal.

e. R^2, the coefficient of determination, will be displayed in cell N5. It shows the percentage of variation in overhead costs that is explained by the change in the volume of the independent variable.

f. Use the portions of the mixed cost developed in d above and next year's estimate of production units in cell C33 to calculate the estimated overhead expense for next year in **cell E33**. (Remember the fixed portion in E32 is a monthly amount.)

3. Use the figures developed in #2 to estimate the overhead expenses Like Magic would have calculated for each of the last 24 months. Develop estimated overhead values by creating formulas in **cells E6-E29**. Use the actual production units for each month and the figures you computed for the variable and fixed portions of overhead, cells E31-E32.

4. Use Excel to plot the regression line through the points you developed in #3 above. The method is similar to assignment 3-A, part 6. Use the same chart and add another new series. Name this series **Regression**. View the graph you have created and make any additional changes that you desire.

5. Repeat steps 2-4 above using labor hours as the independent variable. For this regression the input range for X is **F6:F29**, the input range for Y remains the same, and the output range changes to **M20-U37**. Complete the **column H** figures from the regression results for labor hours. Revise the graph settings for labor hours.

6. Repeat steps 2-4 for machine hours. The output range changes to **M39-U56**.

7. Save your results again in the file **ESTIMATR**.

8. Print your results and your graphs.

9. Compare and comment on the use of the three independent variables for estimating overhead costs. Which variable would you recommend and why? Could Like Magic use

multiple regression? What would be the advantage of using multiple regression versus simple linear regression?

OPTIONAL REQUIREMENTS

Suggest additional data gathering and/or analysis that might be done by Like Magic. Use goodness of fit, economic plausibility, significance of the independent variables, and specification analysis to discuss which of the independent variable should be chosen for cost estimation.

D. COMPUTER INFORMATION

1. Name of the file to be retrieved: **ESTIMATR**
2. Name of the file to save results: **ESTIMATR**
3. Cell locations for results: **E6-E35, H6-H35, K6-K35**

E. WORKSHEET 3: Analysis of Cost Behavior and Cost Estimation

Graphs of Overhead Costs vs. Production Units, Labor Hours, and Machine Hours

F. CHECK FIGURES

	Figures	Cell Location
Prod. Units - Variable Portion	1.98	E31
Machine Hours – Next year Estimate	7067	K33
Jan. Regression Estimate – Prod. Units	448	E6

Worksheet 3 Like Magic Company

COST BEHAVIOR AND COST ESTIMATION

Last 2 Years	Actual Overhead Expense	Production Units - Actual Prod. Units	Production Units - Estimated High Low	Production Units - Regression	Labor Hours - Actual Labor Hours	Labor Hours - Estimated High Low	Labor Hours - Regression	Machine Hours - Actual Mach. Hours	Machine Hours - Estimated High Low	Machine Hours - Regression
Jan	$445	38			37			38		
Feb	350	24			38			16		
Mar	330	32			36			20		
Apr	436	44			44			38		
May	530	48			48			60		
Jun	540	68			50			68		
Jul	448	72			56			72		
Aug	486	55			50			60		
Sep	460	84			56			68		
Oct	476	92			54			72		
Nov	492	90			58			73		
Dec	580	48			56			55		
Jan	500	44			57			48		
Feb	440	32			55			46		
Mar	420	38			60			44		
Apr	560	62			58			66		
May	660	93			96			92		
Jun	525	95			78			80		
Jul	660	85			88			90		
Aug	560	76			86			78		
Sep	550	106			88			84		
Oct	555	112			86			86		
Nov	563	105			88			85		
Dec	605	86			90			84		

Variable Portion:
Fixed Portion:
Next year estimate: 1250   1100   1060

Exhibit 3A   **Like Magic Company**

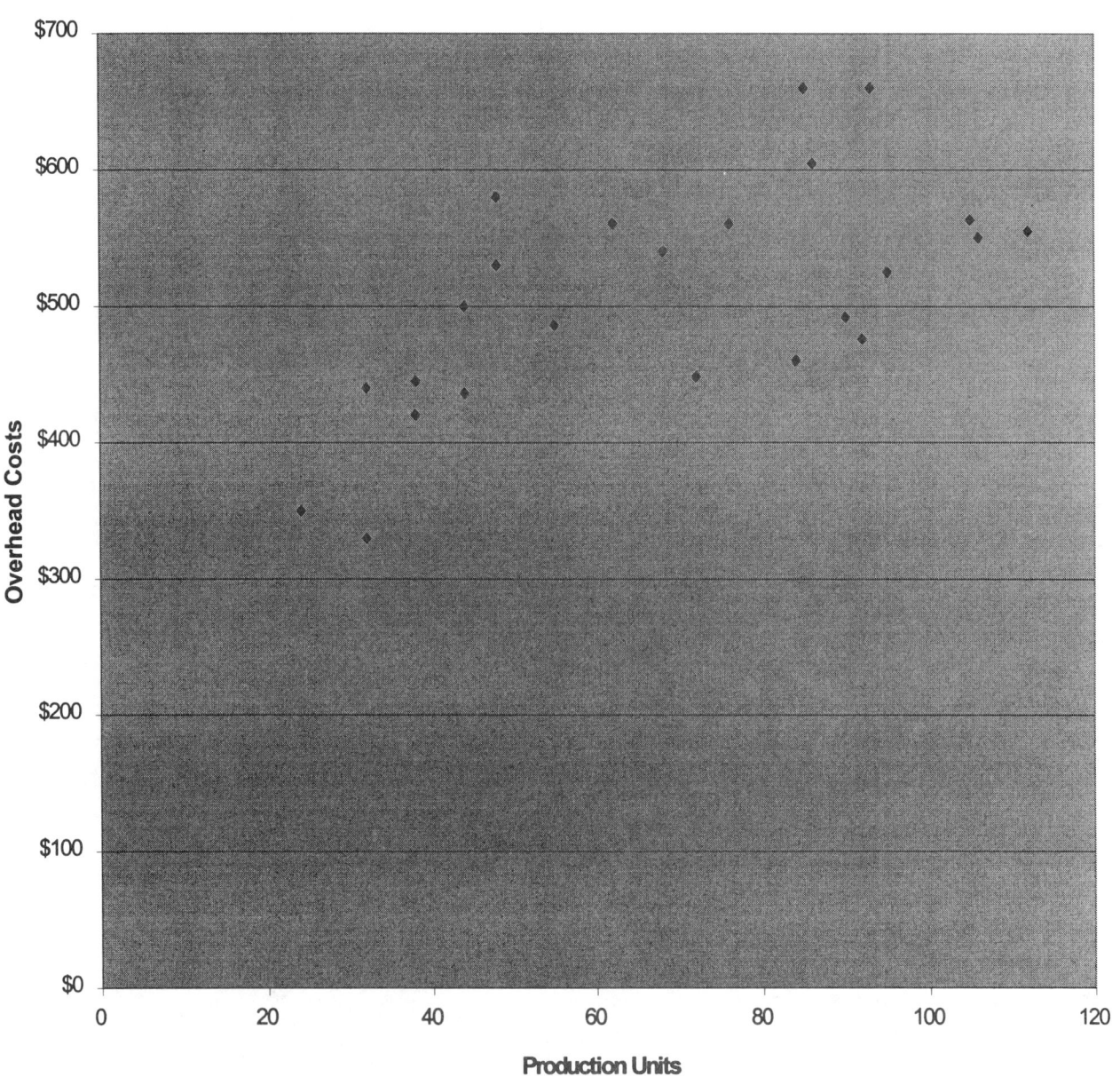

Exhibit 3B   **Like Magic Company**

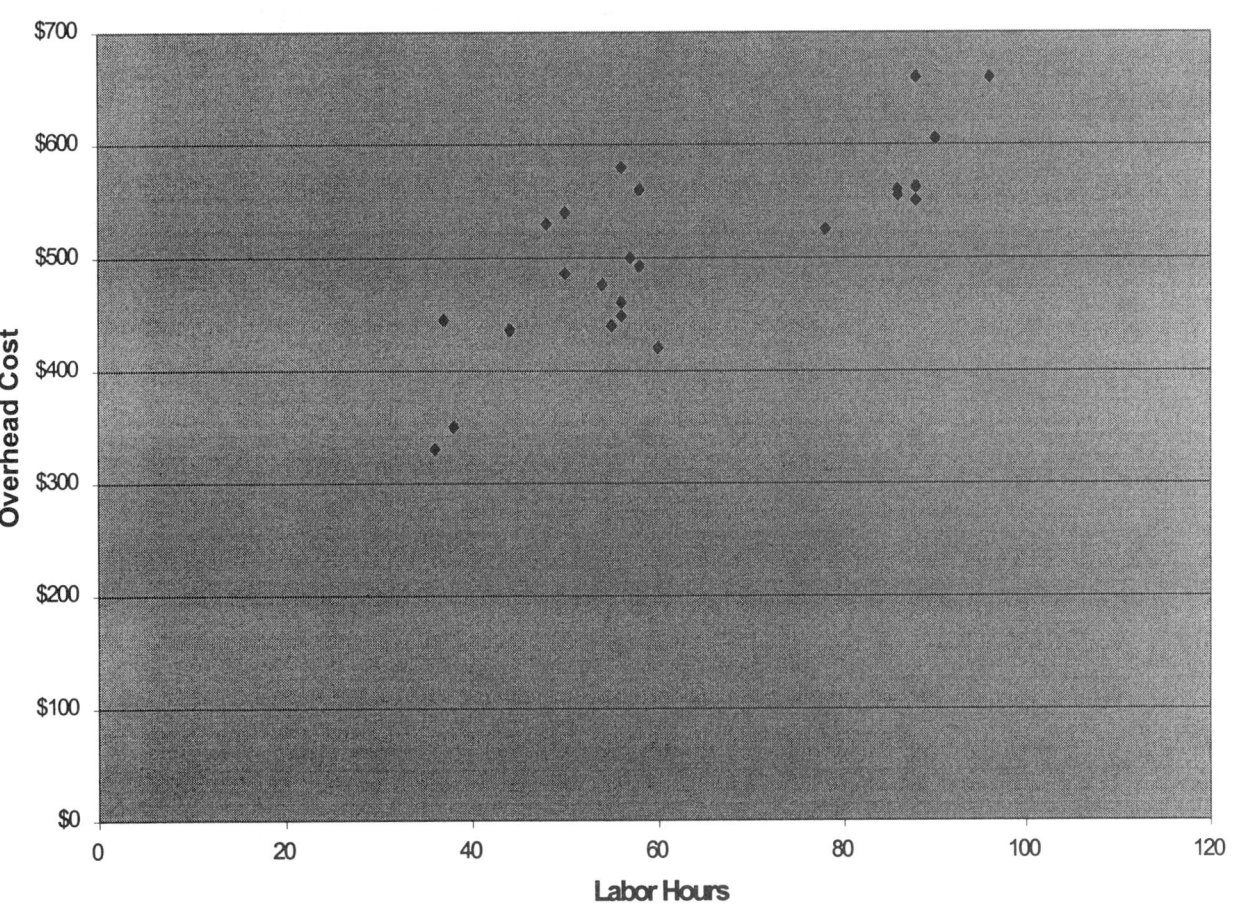

Exhibit 3C   **Like Magic Company**

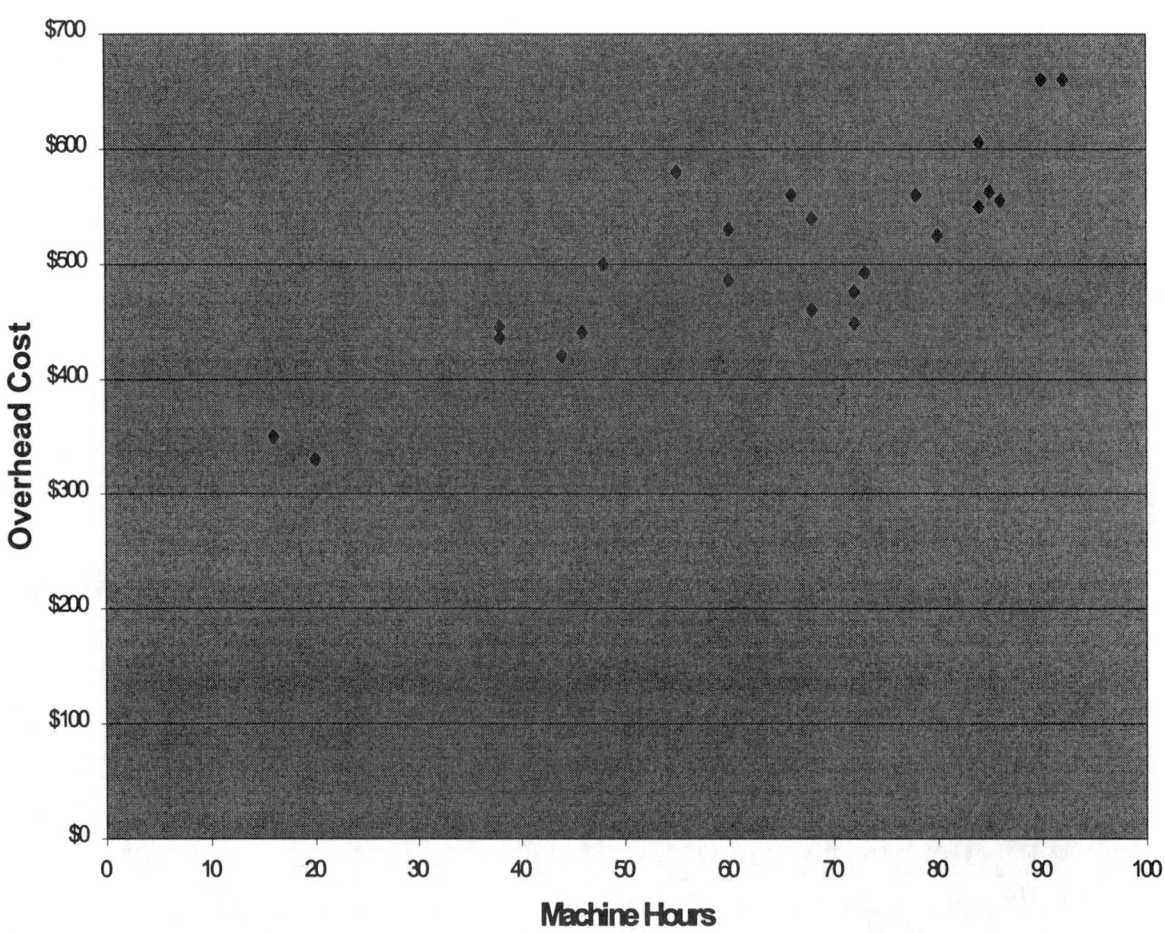

LIKE MAGIC COMPANY

Chapter 4: Cost Management Systems

A: Income Statement – Absorption Approach

A. LEARNING OBJECTIVES

1. Learn to create an income statement for a manufacturing firm using the absorption approach.
2. Use an electronic spreadsheet to link a company's financial accounts and their income statement.
3. Compare the effects on a company's income statement from using or not using a just-in-time system with no finished goods inventory.

B. NARRATIVE

Like Magic would like to build an accounting model using Excel. Their objective is to have the model automatically take information from their general ledger accounts and generate their income statement. Entering formulas, not figures, in the cells of the statement will link the statement to the general ledger data. This link through formulas will allow any changes to data in the general ledger to be automatically adjusted in the statement.

Like Magic is considering a just-in-time production system. Their goal is to have zero inventories, because inventory is a non-value-added activity and there is a substantial cost to own and store inventory. The Turners admire companies such as Dell Computer Corporation who ship as soon as production is complete.

C. REQUIREMENTS

1. Review Worksheet 4. Determine which accounts should be used to complete each line in the absorption income statement. Note the sequential flow between the general ledger accounts and statement. Write in the figures for a few of the lines on Worksheet 4 to make sure that you understand the flow of data.

2. Go to the computer and use Excel to retrieve the file **INCOME**.

3. Use Excel and Like Magic's current year data to complete the income statement when the just-in-time (JIT) system is in use, i.e., when finished-goods inventories = 0. Enter formulas in rows 31-48, columns B-D, to complete the income statement. (See the text for the format of the income statement.) If you want a number that is in one cell to appear in a second cell, in the second cell enter a + and the first cell's location. For example, if you want the sales revenue data in cell C4 to also be shown in cell D31, then **in cell D31 enter +C4**. By maximizing the use of formulas you will greatly ease and speed changes and

recalculations. (See D. Computer Information for help with splitting the screen into two windows so it is easier to enter the formulas.) The income tax rate to be used is in B26.

4. Complete a second version of the income statement when the just-in-time system is not in use. Use the finished-goods inventories in cells C28 and C29. This income statement should go into columns E-G, rows 31-48, starting with sales revenue in cell **G31**.

5. Print your statement. Before the report is printed, insert your name in the Print Header Line. (See Print Header Line in Chapter 1 for instructions.)

6. Save your results in file **INCOMER**.

7. Compare the income when a JIT is in use and not in use. Why is the income different? What could have caused this difference? Is Like Magic more or less profitable because of inventories? Why do companies want to install a JIT? Discuss times or situations when a JIT might have negative effects.

8. Would a cost system like you have developed help Like Magic to better understand their value chain? Why?

D. COMPUTER INFORMATION

1. Name of the file to be retrieved: **INCOME**
2. Name of the file to save results: **INCOMER**
3. Cell location for results: **B31-G48**

Splitting the Screen Into Two Windows

Click the mouse pointer in the left column of the screen in row 14 (any row will do.) Click on **Window** in the top menu bar. Click on **Split** in the drop-down menu. The screen will split into two windows. Use the down arrow in the bottom right side of the screen to scroll down in the bottom window until the Absorption Income Statement is at the top of the lower window. Use the mouse pointer to switch between the upper and lower windows. Each window has its own set of arrows on the right side to scroll up and down.

When you have completed the income statement, use the mouse pointer to click on **Window** again in the top menu bar, and click on **Remove Split** in the drop-down menu. The entire screen will become one window again.

E. WORKSHEET 4 – COST BEHAVIOR AND INCOME STATEMENTS

The objective of this worksheet is to help you understand accounting cost flows through an electronic spreadsheet model. Accounting cost flows are linked in the model by having the same accounts and accompanying dollar amounts appear in two or more schedules, statements or tables. After filling in the worksheet you should be better able to use Excel to complete the formulas for the schedules and statement.

F. CHECK FIGURES

Net Income = $ 2,389 in cell D48

LIKE MAGIC COMPANY

Chapter 4-B: Income Statement – Contribution Approach
Variable and Fixed Costs per Unit
International Aspects of Labor Cost Content

A. LEARNING OBJECTIVES

1. Learn to create an income statement for a manufacturing firm using the contribution approach.
2. Show that unit costs are average costs and distinguish between fixed costs per unit and variable costs per unit.
3. Optional discussion of the affects of labor cost content on income taxes in international locations.

B. NARRATIVE

Like Magic has been growing very rapidly and the Turners have been surprised at how expenses have varied from their forecasts. Tom and Tracy are planning to hold a meeting with their staff to review control of expenses for the past year. They want everyone to understand the impact of changes in sales demand on operating income. Tom is concerned about Like Magic's coming plans for fixed cost investment in automated equipment. Separating variable from fixed costs should help everyone focus on the expense comparisons for the past year. The contribution approach will show the effect of the range of sales on coverage of the new fixed cost investment. The table you'll develop will demonstrate how fixed indirect manufacturing cost per unit will vary significantly as the number of units vary.

C. REQUIREMENTS

1. Retrieve or continue to work with the file **INCOMER**.

2. Review Worksheet 4 again. Determine which accounts should be used to complete each line in the contribution income statement. Note the sequential flow between the general ledger accounts and statement. Write in the figures for a few of the lines on Worksheet 4 to make sure that you understand the flow of data.

3. Use Excel and Like Magic's current year data to complete the income statement, **C50-D69**.

4. Complete the **Unit Cost Change Table, B70-F73**.

a. Calculate the unit cost assigned to direct material, **B72**, using the current year's direct material used and the units manufactured, B71. Use this direct material unit cost for the year to determine the direct material unit cost for each of the four quarters, **C72-F72**. Assume the **total** direct material cost is variable, i.e., it changes each quarter in direct proportion to the number of units manufactured.

b. Calculate the unit cost assigned to fixed indirect manufacturing unit cost for the total year, **B73**, using the figures from the contribution income statement and the units manufactured. Use this total year fixed indirect manufacturing unit cost to determine the unit cost for each of the four quarters, **C73-F73**. Assume the total year fixed indirect manufacturing cost, shown in the contribution income statement, can be divided into equal amounts for each quarter, i.e., it is incurred evenly throughout the year and remains **unchanged** as the number of units manufactured varies.

5. Print your contribution income statement and unit cost change table.

6. Save your results in the file **INCOMER**.

7. Would a company want an absorption or a contribution income statement, or both? What is the value of each and when would each be used? Who would use each and how would they be used?

8. Are the changes in unit costs among the quarters the same for direct material and fixed indirect manufacturing? What is causing the pattern of change that is seen? What value would it be to management to see these changes?

OPTIONAL REQUIREMENTS

Suppose Like Magic moves to a foreign country that offers substantial income tax savings to companies that locate their factories there. For a company to qualify for the income tax savings, its direct labor must exceed 40% of its total manufacturing costs. Discuss how Like Magic might classify the composition of its labor costs to qualify for the income tax savings. You could develop a small table in your spreadsheet to compare alternatives.

D. COMPUTER INFORMATION

1. Name of the file to be retrieved: **INCOME**
2. Name of the file to save results: **INCOMER**
3. Cell location for results: **B50-C69, B71-F73**

E. WORKSHEET 4 – COST BEHAVIOR AND INCOME STATEMENTS

F. CHECK FIGURES

Net Income = $ 2,389 in cell C69

Worksheet 4 Like Magic Company

COST BEHAVIOR AND INCOME STATEMENTS

Accounts: sales, costs, & expenses	Current Year	Cost Behavior V-variable, F-Fixed
Sales revenue	$35,185	V
Interest income	448	V
Direct material used	7,024	V
Direct labor	8,929	V
Indirect labor	808	V
Fringe benefits	1,102	V
Mfg. supplies	132	V
Mfg. power and heat	92	V
Mfg. repairs & maintenance	200	V
Mfg. management salaries	1,495	F
Mfg. building & equipment depreciation	1,880	F
Mfg. insurance	120	F
Mfg. property taxes	648	F
Shipping expenses	840	V
Sales commissions	1,272	V
Marketing salaries	2,667	F
Advertising expenses	2,449	F
Temporary administrative labor	62	V
Administrative salaries	1,509	F
Administrative expenses	150	F
Admin. equipment depreciation	84	F
Interest expenses	550	F
Income taxes: tax rate>	34%	

Just-in-time system --->	In use	Not in use
Finished-goods beginning inventory	$0	$1,050
Finished-goods ending inventory	0	1,350

Absorption Income Statement	JIT system in use	JIT system not in use
Sales revenue		
Finished-goods beginning inventory		
Less costs of goods sold		
Direct material		
Direct labor		
Indirect manufacturing		
Total manufacturing costs		
Finished-goods ending inventory		
Gross profit (gross margin)		
Selling expenses		
Administrative expenses		
Total selling + administrative expenses		
Operating income		
Interest income		
Interest expenses		
Net income before taxes		
Income taxes		
Net income		

Worksheet 4

Like Magic Company

Contribution Income Statement					
Sales revenue					
Less: variable expenses					
Direct material					
Direct labor					
Indirect manufacturing					
Selling expenses					
Administrative expenses					
Total variable expenses					
Contribution margin					
Less: fixed expenses					
Indirect manufacturing					
Selling expenses					
Administrative expenses					
Total fixed expenses					
Operating income					
Interest income					
Interest expenses					
Net income before taxes					
Income taxes					
Net income					
UNIT COST CHANGE TABLE	Total Yr	Qtr 1	Qtr 2	Qtr 3	Qtr 4
Units Manufactured	1,100	214	250	300	336
Direct Material Unit Cost					
Fixed Manufacturing Overhead Unit Cost					

LIKE MAGIC COMPANY

Chapter 5: Relevant Costs for Decision Making

A: Special Sales Orders

A. LEARNING OBJECTIVES

1. Learn to focus on the costs that are relevant in decision making.
2. Use an electronic spreadsheet to develop a decision model for evaluating a special order.
3. Accept or reject a special order using the contribution approach.

B. NARRATIVE

Fawn Fonda, Like Magic's Vice President of Marketing, is sitting in her office telling you about the special request she recently received from The Wizards of the North, a Canadian mail order company. The Wizards want to buy 50,000 jars of Like Magic's cream for a special promotion they plan to run. The Wizards have never been a customer of Like Magic. Fawn is interested in the order especially since Like Magic is considering expanding the market areas where they sell their product. Canada would be a logical market for expanded product distribution.

The Wizards have offered to pay $25.00 per unit for the 50,000 jars. Additional labeling and packaging would increase Like Magic's material costs to $7.00 per jar. The Wizards want Like Magic to perform a final product test before shipment to give assurance that the product is hypoallergenic. Like Magic estimates special equipment, set up and other costs associated with the requested testing would cost $200,000. This cost would not vary significantly even with moderate changes in volume of the special order. There should not be any other fixed costs or variable marketing expenses to manufacture and fill this order. Variable labor expenses and variable manufacturing overhead per unit would be the same as Like Magic's current product. Like Magic has sufficient capacity to produce this order in time for its requested shipment date and still meet their scheduled production.

Fawn has asked for your assistance with this special order from The Wizards of the North. She wants to know whether it would be profitable for Like Magic to accept this order.

C. REQUIREMENTS

1. Review Worksheet 5. The top section presents the data they used in planning for the current year and the data for the special order. The second section of the Worksheet will be used to develop comparative predictive income statements to help evaluate the profitability of the special order. The remaining sections will be used for assignment B and C.

2. Use Excel to open the file **DECIDE**.

3. Create formulas to complete the **Contribution Margin Income Statement** for Like Magic without the special order, **cells B20-B33;** the special order, **cells C20-C33**; and the sum of these two sets of figures, **cells D20-D33**. Use Like Magic's planned sales, selling price and expenses given in cells B5-B15, and the special order data given in cells C5-C15

4. Indicate your answer to Fawn Fonda on whether the special order is profitable by entering a **Yes** or a **No** in **cell C34**.

5. Print the spreadsheet with your results. Before the report is printed, insert your name in the Print Header Line. (See Print Header Line in Chapter 1.)

6. Save your results in the file DECIDER.

D. COMPUTER INFORMATION

1. Name of the file to be retrieved: **DECIDE**
2. Name of the file to save results: **DECIDER**
3. Cell locations for results: **B20-D34**

E. WORKSHEET 5: Relevant Costs for Special Pricing Decisions

F. CHECK FIGURES

	Figures	Cell Locations
Contribution Margin - Without Order	$20,988	B27
Operating Income – Special Order	232	C33

27

LIKE MAGIC COMPANY

Chapter 5: Relevant Costs for Decision Making

B: Cost-plus Pricing and Special Orders

A. LEARNING OBJECTIVES

1. Learn to calculate markup percentages for cost-plus pricing.
2. Develop pricing models using the contribution margin approach.
3. Compare the differing cost-plus pricing models.

B. NARRATIVE

Fawn Fonda wants additional assistance in developing a model for pricing special orders. She would like a price quote table she could use based upon markup percentages. The quote table should range from the minimum price that Like Magic could charge and still not lose money to a target-selling price per unit based upon cost-plus pricing. The table should identify the different markup percentages they might use. Since Fawn will probably negotiate a price with The Wizards, she would like to know what prices Like Magic should charge for this special order if they used prime, variable and full cost bases. Fawn would like these prices without the hypoallergenic final testing since she will charge The Wizards the full cost of the testing without a markup.

C. REQUIREMENTS

1. Review Worksheet 5 again. The next two sections will be used to complete this requirement.

2. Retrieve or continue working with the file **DECIDE**.

3. Complete the **Cost-plus Markup Percentages to Achieve Same Sales Price**.

a. Enter formulas in **cells B37-B42**, to determine per unit sales price, various costs and operating income. These figures should be taken from the current year data without the special order.

b. Enter a formula in **cell C38** to compute the markup on prime costs, cell B38, to achieve the sales price per unit, cell B37. (See the text if you are unsure of the formula.) Next, compute a markup on variable cost by entering a formula in **cell C39**. Finally, compute a markup on total (full or fully allocated) cost by entering a formula in **cell C41**.

4. Complete the **Quote Sheet for Pricing Special Orders**. Enter formulas in **cells B45-B48**, to calculate the target prices that Like Magic might consider charging for this special order. Remember to omit the cost for the special testing since that will be charged separately.

5. Print the spreadsheet with your results.

6. Save your results again in the file **DECIDER**.

OPTIONAL REQUIREMENTS

7. Discuss the advantages and disadvantages to Like Magic of taking on the costs and giving the assurances related to the hypoallergenic testing for this special order.

8. Describe a price negotiation strategy for Like Magic to take with The Wizards of the North for this special order. Discuss the pros and cons for the differing cost plus pricing strategies.

9. What other issues should be evaluated by Like Magic in determining their price negotiation strategy?

D. COMPUTER INFORMATION

1. Name of the file to be retrieved: **DECIDE**
2. Name of the file to save results: **DECIDER**
3. Cell locations for results: **B37-D42 and B45-B48**

E. WORKSHEET 5: Relevant Costs for Special Pricing Decisions

F. CHECK FIGURES

	Figures	Cell Locations
Prime costs / unit	$13.60	B38
Price quote - variable cost / unit	$31.44	B46

LIKE MAGIC COMPANY

Chapter 5: Relevant Costs for Decision Making

C. Optimal Use of Limited Resources

A. LEARNING OBJECTIVES

1. Learn what information is relevant when resources are constrained.
2. Develop a decision model for maximizing total profit when a factor of production is limited.

B. NARRATIVE

Like Magic has just received a new order for 100,000 jars of their regular product. This new order will not cause any of the planned current year's costs to change from those given in assignment A. Like Magic would also like to start manufacturing a new product. The new product will add ingredients to their regular cream giving it a sun block with an SPF of 15. Management plans for the new product include a sales price increase of $5, variable expense increase of $1 and no change in fixed expenses.

At present, Like Magic cannot manufacture enough cream for the planned sales of their regular product, plus the sale of the new product and fill the new order. They do not have enough machine hours available in a key production process. New equipment cannot be purchased and put into use fast enough to help with this situation. Since Like Magic will satisfy their planned sales first, evaluate whether selling the new product or the new order will maximize total profits.

REQUIREMENTS

1. Review Worksheet 5 again. The bottom section is for information when using scarce resources.

2. Create formulas to complete the **Optimal Use of Limited Resources** section of the worksheet. Enter formulas to compute the contribution margin per unit and per hour for the new order and new product, **cells C55-E56**.

3. Which choice is more profitable for Like Magic, accepting the new order or making and selling the new product? Enter a **Yes** in either **cell C57 or E57**.

4. Discuss the advantages and disadvantages of the decision you recommended above.

5. Print the spreadsheet with your results.

6. Save your results in the file **DECIDER**.

D. COMPUTER INFORMATION

1. Name of the file to be retrieved: **DECIDER**
2. Name of the file to save results: **DECIDER**
3. Cell location for results: **C55-E57**

E. WORKSHEET 5: Relevant Costs for Special Pricing Decisions

F. CHECK FIGURES

	Figures	Cell Location
Contribution Margin per Hour for the New Order	$83.95	C56

Worksheet 5 — Like Magic Company

Relevant Costs for Special Pricing Decisions

	Current Year	Special Order
Sales in Units	1,250	50
Selling Price	$35.00	$25.00
Variable Expenses / Unit		
Direct Material	$6.40	$7.00
Direct Labor	7.20	7.20
Manufacturing Overhead	2.16	2.16
Marketing & Administrative	2.45	
Total Fixed Expenses		
Manufacturing Overhead	$4,800	$200
Marketing	5,456	
Administrative	1,980	

Contribution Margin Income Statement

	Without Special Order	Special Order	With Special Order
Sales			
Less: variable expenses			
Direct Material			
Direct Labor			
Manufacturing Overhead			
Marketing & Administrative			
Total variable expenses			
Contribution Margin			
Less: fixed expenses			
Manufacturing Overhead			
Marketing			
Administrative			
Total fixed expenses			
Operating Income			
Decision -------->			

Cost-Plus Markup Percenages to Achieve Same Sales Price

Sales price / unit	
Prime costs / unit (material + labor)	<--Markup %
Variable cost / unit	<--Markup %
Fixed cost / unit	
Total full cost / unit	<--Markup %
Operating Income / unit	

Quote Sheet for Pricing Special Orders

- Basis: prime costs / unit
- Basis: variable cost / unit
- Basis: full cost / unit
- Minimum price / unit

Optimal Use of Limited Resources

	New Order	New Product
Sales price / unit	No change	+ $5
Variable cost / unit	No change	+ $1
Fixed cost	No change	No change
Units Produced per Hour	5	3
Contribution Margin per Unit		
Contribution Margin per Hour		
** Decision ---->		

LIKE MAGIC COMPANY

Chapter 6: Relevant Costs for Make or Buy Decision Making

A. LEARNING OBJECTIVES

1. Learn to focus on the costs that are relevant in decision making.
2. Use an electronic spreadsheet to develop decision models for evaluating a make or buy decision with income potential from alternative use of idle facilities.
3. Identify relevant costs, opportunity costs, postponable costs and sunk costs.

B. NARRATIVE

Tracy Turner has decided Like Magic could increase their revenue and profit by also selling their cream in an upscale designer jar at a higher price. Tracy had the jar designed and the staff developed projected data for the upscale jar of cream. The proposed selling price was $40 per jar, $5 above the price of the current jar. Demand was projected at 100,000 jars for the coming year. Material expenses would be $1 per jar greater than for their regular product. The other variable expenses would be the same per unit cost as their current product. Fixed manufacturing overhead expenses would be $600,000. Fixed marketing expenses for advertising and promotion for the designer jar would cost an additional $300,000.

Anthony Iococca, Vice President of Manufacturing, suggested they consider purchasing the jar from an outside manufacturer for the first year. This would let Like Magic test the results of the new jar before investing funds in production equipment. If they bought the jar, Like Magic could avoid $200,000 in fixed manufacturing overhead. Anthony said idle space is available if they decide to manufacture the new jar. He added that a request had been received from another firm to rent storage facilities from Like Magic for the coming year. If the jar was purchased from another manufacturer, the space could be rented for $50,000 for the next year.

Tom Turner has received a request for Like Magic to do some contract manufacturing of a cream similar to theirs. He asks the staff to evaluate whether the idle space should be used for contract manufacturing if they purchase the designer jar. You roughly estimate the contract manufacturing would yield a $60,000 contribution to profits for the coming year.

Tracy asks you to evaluate the profitability of producing and selling the cream in the designer jar. You set up four alternatives: make the jar, buy the jar outside and keep the space idle, buy the jar outside and rent the available space, buy the jar outside and use the available space for contract manufacturing.

C. REQUIREMENTS

1. Review Worksheet 6. The top section contains the data to be used for making the designer jar and the amounts saved if purchased outside. The outside purchase cost is $3.60 per jar,

the potential rent from the idle space is $50,000, and, if they do the contract manufacturing, the income is shown as $60,000.

2. In the second section of the Worksheet, the four columns are for developing comparative predictive income statements. These columns should be used for the data to make the jar, buy it outside and not rent the idle space, buy the jar outside and rent the space, and buy it outside and use the space for contract manufacturing.

3. Use Excel to open the file **MAKE-BUY**.

4. Create formulas to complete the **Contribution Margin Income Statements** for the four alternatives: make the jar, **cells B21-B36**, buy the jar outside and not rent the idle space, **C21-C36**, buy the jar outside and rent the idle space, **D21-D36**, and buy the jar and use the space for contract manufacturing, **E21-E36**. Use the data presented in cells B4-C16.

5. Indicate which would be the most profitable of the four alternatives by entering a **Yes** in one of the **cells B37, C37, D37 or E37**.

6. Print the spreadsheet with your results. Insert your name in the Print Header Line. (See Print Header Line in Chapter 1.)

7. Save your results.

8. What are the relevant costs among the three alternatives of making or buying the jar?

9. What would the opportunity cost be for Like Magic if they decided to make the jar themselves?

10. Give an example of an avoidable cost from these alternatives.

11. Would any of the building expenses be considered a sunk cost and not have to be included in this analysis?

OPTIONAL REQUIREMENTS

12. What would be the maximum purchase price for the designer jars acceptable to Like Magic? Enter the formula to show the result in **row 38**, under the appropriate column.

13. What non-cost factors should Like Magic consider when deciding whether to sell the designer product? What are some of the issues affecting Like Magic in choosing among the four alternatives of making or buying the designer jar?

14. How would the profitability among the alternatives change if the estimated sales were 200,000 units of the designer product? (You can save time by using a **copy** then **paste-values** with the work you have done. The following directions use the right mouse button, instead you could use edit from the menu at the top of the screen. First **select cells A17-E38:** move the pointer to cell A17, press and hold the left mouse button, then

drag the pointer to cell E38 and release. Cells A17-E38 should be highlighted. Press the right mouse button and **select copy** from the drop-down menu. **Select cell A39:** move the pointer to cell A39 and press the left mouse button. Press the right mouse button. Then **select paste-special** from the drop-down menu. **Select values** from the menu. Then **select OK**. Excel should have copied all the data but not the formulas you developed to the lower cells in your spreadsheet. Go back to the top and **change the sales in units to 200**. Excel should automatically recalculate the income statements if you used formulas to create the statements. Next **move the decision and maximum purchase price in rows 37 and 38 to the appropriate cells.**)

D. COMPUTER INFORMATION

1. Name of the file to be retrieved: **MAKE-BUY**
2. Name of the file to save results: **MAKEBUYR**
3. Cell location for results: **B21-E38, B43-E60.**

E. WORKSHEET 6: Relevant Costs for Make or Buy Decisions

F. CHECK FIGURES

	Figures	Cell Location
Contribution margin: make the jar	$2,079	B29
Total income: buy – keep space idle	$1,245	C36

Worksheet 6 — Like Magic Company

Relevant Costs for Make or Buy Decisions

	Make	Changes if Buying
Sales in units	100	
Selling price	$40.00	
Variable expenses / unit		
Direct material	$7.40	($1.40)
Direct labor	7.20	(0.70)
Manufacturing overhead	2.16	(0.16)
Marketing & administrative	2.45	
Total fixed expenses		
Manufacturing overhead	$600	($200)
Marketing	300	
Outside purchase cost per unit		$3.60
Rent income from idle space		50
Contract income from idle space		60

Contribution Margin Income Statement

Sales in units ----->	100 Make	Buy Space Idle	Buy Space Rented	Buy Space Use for Contract
Sales				
Less: variable expenses				
Direct material				
Direct labor				
Manufacturing overhead				
Marketing & administrative				
Outside purchase				
Total variable expenses				
Contribution margin				
Less: fixed expenses				
Manufacturing overhead				
Marketing				
Total fixed expenses				
Operating income				
Rent/contract income				
Total income				
Decision -------->				
Maximum price-buy outside				

Worksheet 6   Like Magic Company

Sales in units -----> Contribution Margin Income Statement	200 Make	Buy Space Idle	Buy Space Rented	Buy Space Use for Contract
Sales				
Less: variable expenses				
Direct material				
Direct labor				
Manufacturing overhead				
Marketing & administrative				
Outside purchase				
Total variable expenses				
Contribution margin				
Less: fixed expenses				
Manufacturing overhead				
Marketing				
Total fixed expenses				
Operating income				
Rent/contract income				
Total income				
Decision -------->				
Maximum price-buy outside				

LIKE MAGIC COMPANY

Chapter 7: Budgeting

A: Operating Budget

A. LEARNING OBJECTIVES

1. Gain understanding of budgeting.
2. Learn to use a sales forecast as the starting point for budget preparation.
3. Use an electronic spreadsheet to prepare sales, production, purchases, cost of goods sold, marketing and administrative expenses, and income statement budgets.
4. Demonstrate how changes in sales forecasts, planned ending inventories, and/or expenses affect budgeted figures.

B. NARRATIVE

The management of Like Magic is enthusiastic about your spreadsheets. Tracy Turner wants to develop and review an operating budget based upon the most profitable income projection. Tracy suggests that by developing this budget, the staff will better understand the relationships among the key operating and decision variables affecting operating income. Tracy adds reviewing the budget figures will provide a more realistic assessment of the likelihood of achieving those figures. Tom Turner says he would like to see a budget based upon a less optimistic forecast. This will enable the firm to see the impact of an economic downturn or increased competition. The staff responds favorably to the cooperative budget development. They feel cooperation will lead to coordinated effort to achieve common goals as well as uncovering potential problems before they occur.

You decide to develop the budget using an electronic spreadsheet model because of the ease of testing various assumptions and the likelihood of several budget revisions. You know Like Magic's management will want to examine several "what if" situations before choosing a final budget.

C. REQUIREMENTS

1. Review Worksheet 7. Note the top section presents estimated data for the coming year. Operating figures are given for the first quarter, and a sales forecast is shown in units by month.

2. Use Excel to open the file **BUDGET**.

3. Complete the budgeted figures starting with the Sales Budget for each of the first three months and the quarter total. End this assignment with the Operating income on the Income Statement. (Assignment 7-B continues with the remaining figures.)

a. Enter formulas to compute the sales budget in $, **cells D19-F19**. Multiply the expected sales in units, **G4-G15**, and multiply by the selling price, in **B4**.

b. Enter formulas to complete the production budget. The finished goods ending inventory for the end of the prior quarter 4 is given in C22. The requirement for planned finished goods ending inventories is in row 9. (Hint: remember units to be produced = expected sales + required finished goods ending inventory - finished goods beginning inventory.)

c. Enter formulas to complete the purchase budget. The standards for pounds of material per unit and price per pound of material are given in row 5. The requirement for planned raw material ending inventories is in row 10.

d. Complete the cost of goods sold budget. The budget figures for cost of goods manufacturing are given. The value for finished goods ending inventories should be equal to the units for finished goods ending inventories in the production budget times the total standard product cost, cell B7.

e. Complete the budgets for marketing and general and administrative expenses. Supporting figures are given in B12-B15. Figures for December of the prior year are given in C40-C46.

f. Complete the income statement through operating income.

g. Compute the budget figures for the total quarter, G19-G56.

4. Print the budgeted schedules and income statement. Insert your name in the Print Header Line. (See Print Header Line in Chapter 1.)

5. Save your results in the file **BUDGETR**.

D. COMPUTER INFORMATION

1. Name of the file to be retrieved: **BUDGET**
2. Name of the file to save results: **BUDGETR**
3. Cell locations for results: D19-G61

E. WORKSHEET 7: Master Budget

F. CHECK FIGURES

	Figures	Cell Location
Sales budget in $ for January	$3290	D19
Units to be produced for Quarter 1	289	G25
Operating Income for January	$ 602	D56

39

LIKE MAGIC COMPANY

Chapter 7-B: Cash Budget

A. LEARNING OBJECTIVES

1. Gain understanding of the relationship among cash collections, cash disbursements, minimum cash balances and short term financing.
2. Learn to prepare a cash budget including a financing section for borrowing and repayments.

B. NARRATIVE

The Turners liked the budgeted schedules and income statement you prepared. Tracy would like to expand the budgeted data to see a cash budget. Ruby Rockefeller, their friendly banker, advised Tom to request a line of credit for short term financing well in advance of when Like Magic might need extra cash. Ruby said the bank would like to see budgeted statements and a cash projection, at the time Like Magic asks for the line of credit.

Before developing the cash budget, you reviewed the history of cash collections and disbursements. You also spoke with management, customers, vendors, and the bank about the policy of each regarding cash related activity. The summary of this information is presented in the spreadsheet section entitled "Estimated Cash, Financing and Other Expense Information." That information is expanded upon as each requirement is discussed in section C. Requirements. Some simplification has been made to ease the number of calculations.

Having collected the cash related information, you are ready to expand your electronic spreadsheet to prepare the cash budget. You want to be sure the data on all the budgeted forms are interrelated by making the cell entries formulas. These interrelationships will ease and speed recalculations when you change some of the starting assumptions.

C. REQUIREMENTS

1. Retrieve or continue working with the file **BUDGETR**.

2. Review the section on Estimated Cash, Financing and Other Expense Information, rows 62-79.

3. Enter formulas to complete the Cash Collections Budget for the first three months of the year and the quarter total, **cells C81-F85**. Assume that all sales are on credit, there are no discounts for prompt payment and that all credit amounts are collected. Use the company's history that 50% of the sales on credit are collected in the month of the sale and the remaining 50% are collected in the month following the sale. The accounts receivable for the prior yearend is shown. (The prior year-end accounts receivable is high because of a

sales promotion that Like Magic ran which granted extended payment terms on the amounts owed.)

4. Enter formulas to complete the cash available section of the cash budget. Cash is received monthly on investment interest income. This investment income is based upon the amount of long-term investments on the prior year-end amount, shown in the balance sheet, row 119, and the annual interest income rate given in cell B75.

5. Enter formulas to complete the cash disbursement section of the cash budget.

a. All material purchased in a month are included in accounts payable and are paid for in the following month. Thus, the January payment for material purchases would be the prior year-end accounts payable, cell C125.

b. All wages and salaries earned in a month are paid in the same month. Sales commissions earned in a month become commissions payable at the end of the month and are paid in the following month. The cash payment for any month of labor, salaries and commissions equals manufacturing, marketing and administrative labor and salaries plus sales commissions for the prior month. The sales commissions payable for December of the prior year is shown in the balance sheet.

c. The cash payment for other current liabilities for January is equal to the other current liabilities for the prior yearend shown in the balance sheet. The cash payment for other current liabilities for February and March are given in cells B68. Other current liabilities include amounts for interest, taxes, insurance, supplies, etc.

d. Dividends are paid quarterly in the first month of the following quarter, e.g., fourth quarter dividends payable on 12/31 are paid in January.

e. Like Magic is planning to purchase a building and equipment in January. The building cost of $2,000,000 will be an addition to long-term debt. The equipment will be purchased with a cash payment of $4,000,000. Depreciation of this equipment has already been included in the budgeted fixed manufacturing overhead.

f. Like Magic will increase their long-term investment with a cash payment of $1,000,000 in January. This investment will not effect interest income in the first quarter.

6. Complete the cash excess or deficiency. The minimum cash balance desired is given in cell B77.

7. Enter formulas to complete the financing section of the cash budget including the ending cash balance. Any cash deficiency will be covered by short term borrowing with notes payable to the bank. Cash borrowing is equal to the amount of any cash deficiency for a month and is made at the beginning of the month. Any cash excess for a month is first used to pay the interest owed on any short term borrowing and then to pay back as much as possible of the short term borrowing. Assume cash payments are made at the end of a month. The interest is based upon the annual interest rate given in cell B74.

8. Print the cash budget.

9. Save your results in the file **BUDGETR**.

D. COMPUTER INFORMATION

1. Name of the file to be retrieved: **BUDGETR**
2. Name of the file to save results: **BUDGETR**
3. Cell location for results: **C81-F107**

E. WORKSHEET 7: Master Budget

F. CHECK FIGURES

	Figures	Cell Location
Cash collections for January	$5,929	C85
Total cash available for January	7,949	C90
Cash deficiency for January	(1,252)	C101
Cash effects of financing – February	(385)	D106

LIKE MAGIC COMPANY

Chapter 7-C: A Budgeted Balance Sheet

A. LEARNING OBJECTIVES

1. Use the cash financing information to complete a budgeted income statement and a budgeted balance sheet.
2. Demonstrate the speed and flexibility of electronic spreadsheets to present data under varying planning assumptions.

B. NARRATIVE

The cash budget has proven very beneficial. Tom Turner would like to include the financing on the income statement and have a budgeted balance sheet. Tom wants to see what their cash position might be under varying management decisions and economic conditions.

Having prepared the cash budget, you are ready to expand your electronic spreadsheet to complete the income statement and develop the balance sheet. You want the data on all the budgeted forms to be interrelated by making the cell entries formulas. These interrelationships will ease and speed recalculations when you change some of the starting assumptions.

C. REQUIREMENTS

1. Retrieve or continue working with the file **BUDGETR**.

2. Enter formulas to complete the income statement. Investment interest income was calculated in the cash budget. Interest expense is the interest due on total non-current liabilities plus short term financing. Interest on non-current liabilities is based upon the interest rate on financing and the total of non-current liabilities at the end of the prior quarter or year. For simplicity, the interest expense on financing is shown in the month it is paid, and interest payable is included in other current liabilities on the balance sheet. The income tax rate is given in B76.

3. Enter formulas to complete the budgeted balance sheet. Prior year-end figures are given in column C. Additional figures for first quarter expenses and prior quarter ending balances are given in the section on Estimated Cash, Financing and Other Expense Information. Notes payable should come from the Cash Budget and will be equal to cash borrowing minus repayments. Dividends of $400 are declared in the third month of each quarter. There are no planned additions to bonds payable or stockholders' equity.

4. Print the budgeted income statement and balance sheet.

5. Save your results in the file **BUDGETR**.

OPTIONAL REQUIREMENTS

6. What would happen to income and cash flows if some of the starting assumptions change? Enter the following changes into your spreadsheet, print the results and comment on the impact on income and cash flow.

   - Sales for January through March are 85,000 units/month.
   - Direct material cost increases to $38 per pound.
   - Cash collected in the month of sale drops to 40%. The 10% drop is due to non-paying accounts.

7. Discuss what Like Magic should do if they think that there is a reasonable likelihood a recession would cause these conditions to occur.

D. COMPUTER INFORMATION

1. Name of the file to be retrieved: **BUDGETR**
2. Name of the file to save results: **BUDGETR**
3. Cell location for results: **E111-E139**

E. WORKSHEET 7: Master Budget

F. CHECK FIGURES

	Figures	Cell Location
Net Income – quarter 1	1,053	G61
Total assets – quarter 1	27,114	E121
Total current liabilities – quarter 1	2,688	E129

Worksheet 7 — Like Magic Company

Master Budget

Estimated Operating Figures - First Quarter

	Price	Per	Amount	Per Unit
Selling price	$35.00	unit		
Direct material	$32.00	lb	0.20	lbs/unit
Direct labor	$12.00	hour	0.60	hrs/unit
Total unit cost	$19.60	unit		

Sales Forecast — Thousands of units

Jan	94
Feb	96
Mar	97
Apr	99
May	101
June	103
July	105
Aug	107
Sept	109
Oct	111
Nov	113
Dec	115
Year	1,250

Planned Ending Inventories:
- Finished goods: 70% Unit sales next month
- Raw material: 150% Material used same month

Marketing, General and Administrative Expense Budgets:
- Sales commissions: 7.0% Sales
- Marketing: salaries & expenses: $20 Increase monthly from Dec.
- General: salaries & expenses: 2% Increase monthly from Dec.
- Office equipment depreciation: $7 per month

Sales Budget - $

	Current Year	Jan.	Feb.	Mar.	Qtr. 1
Sales budget - $					

Production Budget - units

	Qtr.4	Jan.	Feb.	Mar.	Qtr. 1
Expected sales					
Finished goods ending inventory	67				
Production needs					
Finished goods beginning inventory					
Units to be produced					

Purchases Budget - $

	Qtr.4	Jan.	Feb.	Mar.	Qtr. 1
Material usage - pounds					
Raw material ending inventory	28.0				
Material needs - pounds					
Raw material beginning inventory					
Pounds to be purchased					
Purchase cost - material					

Cost of Goods Sold Budget - $

	Qtr.4	Jan.	Feb.	Mar.	Qtr. 1
Finished goods beginning inventory					
Cost of goods manufactured budget		1,795	1,924	1,951	
Cost of goods available					
Finished goods ending inventory	1,350				
Cost of goods sold budget					

Marketing Expense Budget - $

	Dec.	Jan.	Feb.	Mar.	Qtr. 1
Sales commissions	$475				
Marketing salaries	230				
Advertising expenses	203				
Marketing expense budget					

General & Admin. Expense Budget - $

	Dec.	Jan.	Feb.	Mar.	Qtr. 1
General and admin. salaries	$128				
General and admin. expenses	19				
Office equipment depreciation					
General and admin. expense budget					

Income Statement

Next Quarter Ending March 31

	Jan.	Feb.	Mar.	Qtr. 1
Sales				
Cost of goods sold				
Gross profit				
Total marketing expenses				
Total general and admin. expenses				
Operating income				
Investment interest income				
Interest expenses				
Net income before taxes				
Income taxes				
Net income				

Worksheet 7 — Like Magic Company

Estimated Cash, Financing and Other Expense Information

Cash collections- sales	50% Month of sale	50% Following month
Cash payments:		
Material purchases	100% Following month	
Labor and salaries	100% Month of expense	
Sales commissions	100% Following month	
Other current liabilities	$1,036 Paid in February and March	
" " "	$875 Balance: end quarter 1 (3/31)	
Purchase building	$2,000 No cash, all long-term debt	
Purchase equipment	$4,000 All in cash paid in January	
Long term investment	$1,000 All in cash paid in January	
Dividends paid quarterly	$400 Due end of quarter, paid first month the next quarter	
Interest on financing	10% Paid at month-end if cash is available	
Investment interest income rate	8% Investments - long term	
Income tax rate	34%	
Minimum cash balance	$1,000	
Prior year end cash balance	$1,983	
Depreciation	$390 First quarter	

Cash Collections Budget

	Jan.	Feb.	Mar.	Qtr. 1
Accounts receivable: 1/1	$4,284			
January sales				
February sales				
March sales				
Collections from customers				

Cash Budget

	Jan.	Feb.	Mar.	Qtr. 1
Cash balance, beginning				
Collections from customers				
Investment interest income				
Total cash available				
Less disbursements:				
Material purchases				
Labor, salaries & commissions				
Other current liabilities				
Dividends paid				
Purchase equipment				
Investment - long term				
Total disbursements				
Minimum balance desired				
Total cash needed				
Cash excess (deficiency)				
Financing:				
Borrowing: at beginning				
Interest on financing				
Repayments: at end				
Cash effects of financing				
Cash balance, ending				

Worksheet 7

Like Magic Company

Balance Sheet	Prior Year End	Quarter 1 End
Current assets		
Cash	$1,983	
Accounts receivable	4,284	
Raw materials inventory	840	
Finished goods inventory	1,350	_____
Total current assets	$8,457	_____
Non-current assets		
Land	2,000	
Buildings & equipment net	7,904	
Investments - long term	5,600	_____
Total non-current assets	15,504	_____
Total assets	$23,961	
Current liabilities		
Notes payable		
Accounts payable	$632	
Commissions payable	475	
Other current liabilities	636	
Dividends payable	400	
Total current liabilities	$2,143	
Non-current liabilities		
Bonds payable	3,190	
Long-term debt	2,790	
Total non-current liabilities	$5,980	
Stockholders' equity		
Common stock, $1 par value	2,000	
Capital in excess of par	7,960	
Retained earnings	5,878	
Total stockholders' equity	15,838	
Total liability plus stockholders' equity	$23,961	

LIKE MAGIC COMPANY

Chapter 8: Flexible Budgets and Variance Analysis

A: Master and Flexible Budget Variances

A. LEARNING OBJECTIVES

1. Gain understanding of the differences between flexible and master budgets.
2. Learn to construct a flexible budget based upon the level of sales.
3. Use an electronic spreadsheet to compute the flexible budget variances and sales activity variances.
4. Evaluate the company's financial performance using variance analysis.

B. NARRATIVE

In January, a standard costing system was installed at the directive of Tom Turner. Tom wanted to motivate everyone to control costs and improve financial performance. Each manager was responsible for initiating the budget in his or her area, comparing actual results with their budget, and explaining the reasons for the variations. Tom only wanted to get involved when the variations were significant and unexpected. He felt this *management by exception* would have very positive impacts on managers as well as the company.

Tom asked you to develop an activity-based flexible budget using units of product as a single cost driver. He wanted to help Like Magic isolate the causes of variances. It was especially important to distinguish between effectiveness and efficiency while evaluating the financial performance.

You decide to develop a summary performance report using an electronic spreadsheet model. The report will focus on the sales activity variances, the differences between the master and flexible budgets, and the flexible budget variances, the differences between the flexible budget and actual results.

C. REQUIREMENTS

1. Review Worksheet 8. Note the top section presents estimated data for the first quarter. Below the estimated figures the actual pounds of direct material and actual labor hours are listed. Next comes the **Flexible Budget Variance Report** with the actual results shown. Your requirement is to complete the last four columns. The last section for the **Price and Usage Variances Report** will be completed for assignment B.

2. Use Excel to open the file **VARIANCE**.

3. Complete the **Master Budget, cells F17-F31**. Use the units budgeted and the per unit data for sales and variable expenses. For the sales, multiply the units, cell **F17**, by the selling price per unit, cell **B4**.

4. Complete the **Flexible Budget, cells D17-D31**.

5. Compute the **Flexible Budget Variances, cells C17-C31,** and the **Sales Activity Variances, cells E17-E31**.

6. Print the spreadsheet with your results. Insert your name in the Print Header Line. (See Print Header Line in Chapter 1.)

7. Save your results in the file **VARIANCR**.

8. Discuss your results. Why are some figures positive, some negative and some zero? What are possible causes of the sales activity and flexible budget variances? Is it unusual that fixed expense categories can have variances?

D. COMPUTER INFORMATION

1. Name of the file to be retrieved: **VARIANCE**
2. Name of the file to save results: **VARIANCR**
3. Cell locations for results: **B17-F31**

E. WORKSHEET 8: Variance Analysis

F. CHECK FIGURES

	Figures	Cell Location
Master budget sales	$10,045	F18
Flexible budget contribution margin	$ 5,104	D25
Flexible budget variance-direct labor	$ 161	C21

49

LIKE MAGIC COMPANY

Chapter 8-B: Price and Usage Variances

A. LEARNING OBJECTIVES

1. Learn to compute the price and usage variances for a manufacturing firm.
2. Gain understanding of the effects of inventory on material variances.
3. Learn to compute the variable overhead spending and efficiency variances.
4. Understand how to interpret variances and suggest when the variances should be investigated.

B. NARRATIVE

Tom Turner likes your variance presentation. Now he wants to examine the flexible budget variances in more detail. Tom says direct material and direct labor are the largest elements of cost and need to be watched closely. Anthony Iococca reminds Tom the variable factory overhead expenses can often indicate when future cost overruns will occur.

Tom asks you to separate out price and usage variances for direct material and direct labor, as well as the variable indirect factory spending and efficiency variances. After computing the variances, Tom wants you to assist the staff in discussing the possible causes and the trade-off among all of the variances. He would like some rules to use as to when the variances need to be investigated. Tracy Turner asks how the report results would change if actual selling prices were included.

You plan to expand the spreadsheet you developed to compute these variances. You note the direct labor price variance is sometimes called a rate variance and the usage variances can be referred to as quantity or efficiency variances. In a similar fashion, the variable indirect factory spending and efficiency variances can be categorized as price and usage variances.

C. REQUIREMENTS

1. Retrieve or continue working with the file **VARIANCR**.

2. Review the bottom section, the **Price and Usage Variance Report**.

3. Enter formulas to complete the **Direct Material Purchase Price Variance, B38-D40**. Put the variance in **cell C40**. The actual pounds of direct material are in row 12, the actual cost in row 20, and the standards in row 5.

4. Enter formulas to complete the **Direct Material Usage Variance, D41-F43**. Put the variance in **cell E43**.

5. Enter formulas to complete the **Direct Labor Price and Usage Variances, B44-F46**. Put the price variance in **cell C46** and the usage variance in **cell E46**.

6. Enter formulas to complete the **Variable Indirect Factory Price and Usage Variances, B47-F49**. Put the price variance in **cell C49** and the usage variance in **cell E49**.

7. Compute the **Total Flexible Budget Variances** by putting the sum of the price variances in **cell C51**, the sum of the usage variances in **cell E51**, and the sum of the price and usage variances in **cell D52**.

8. Print the variance analysis.

9. Save your results in the file **VARIANCR**.

10. Interpret the results. What may be causing the variances? Is it possible that certain combinations of positive and negative variances might be expected to occur? Should Like Magic do anything about any of these variances? Suppose they have a criterion of investigating any variance that is 6% over or under standard, should they investigate any of their variances?

OPTIONAL REQUIREMENTS

11. What would happen to their results if the actual selling price was different from their estimated price? Recalculate their actual sales using their actual selling price for the quarter of $34.50. Discuss the changes to their variances.

D. COMPUTER INFORMATION

1. Name of the file to be retrieved: **VARIANCR**
2. Name of the file to save results: **VARIANCR**
3. Cell location for results: **B38-F52**

E. WORKSHEET 8: Variance Analysis

F. CHECK FIGURES

	Figures	Cell Location
Direct material purchase price variance	-$ 106	C40
Total flexible budget usage variance	$ 1	E51

Worksheet 8 — Like Magic Company

Variance Analysis

Estimated Operating Figures - First Quarter

	Price	Per	Amount	Per Unit	Budget $ / Unit
Selling price	$35.00	unit			$35.00
Direct material	$32.00	lb	0.2	lbs/unit	$6.40
Direct labor	$12.00	hour	0.6	hrs/unit	$7.20
Variable indirect factory	$3.60	labor hour	0.6	hrs/unit	$2.16
Variable marketing	7%	$ of sales			$2.45
Fixed indirect factory	1,200	per quarter			
Fixed marketing	1,539	per quarter			
Fixed administrative	480	per quarter			
Actual direct material - lbs	63	purchased	62	used	
Actual direct labor - hours	180	used			

Flexible Budget Variances

	Actual Results	Flexible-Budget Variances	Flexible-Budget	Sales-Activity Variances	Master Budget
Units	304				287
Sales	$10,640				
Less: variable expenses					
Direct material	1,910				
Direct labor	2,350				
Indirect factory	680				
Marketing	740				
Total variable expenses	5,680				
Contribution margin	$4,960				
Less: fixed expenses					
Indirect factory	1,200				
Marketing	1,560				
Administrative	472				
Total fixed expenses	3,232				
Operating income	$1,728				

Price and Usage Variances

		Actual Results Actual inputs Actual Prices	Price Variances	Flexible-Budget Actual inputs Expected Prices	Usage Variances	Standard Inputs Allowed Actual outputs Expected Prices
Direct Material Purchase	Quantity---> Price---> Total--->					
Direct Material Usage	Quantity---> Price---> Total--->					
Direct Labor	Hours---> Rate---> Total--->					
Variable Indirect Factory	Hours---> Rate---> Total--->					

Total flexible budget variance

LIKE MAGIC COMPANY

Chapter 9: Control in Decentralized Organizations

A: Performance Measures

A. LEARNING OBJECTIVES

1. Learn how to compute return on investment and residual income.
2. Understand the effect on residual income of using different rates for cost of capital.
3. Demonstrate how judgments on division performance and decisions on new projects are affected by the performance measure chosen as the criterion.
4. Show the effect of using gross versus net book value on ROI and residual income.
5. Explain the effects of using economic value added (EVA) and alternative measures of invested capital.

B. NARRATIVE

Tom Turner, Like Magic's President, is planning to purchase a few firms to expand their size and market share. Tom is deeply involved in negotiations to purchase another firm named Softer which makes a complementary line of cosmetics. Like Magic and Softer would become two divisions under the parent company. Part of the proposed purchase price of Softer would be payments based upon the future performance of Softer. Tom is trying to decide whether to use return on investment (ROI) or residual income as the criterion to evaluate performance. Like Magic is going to have to borrow long-term funds to buy Softer and other firms. Tom is not sure what interest rates they will have to pay on its new liabilities. He would like to see how division performance would change as the rate for cost of capital changes.

Tom is also planning to purchase the rights to produce a new product in the United States that has recently been introduced in Europe. Investment, manufacturing and sales of this new product would be included under the control of either the Like Magic or Softer divisions. Tom is concerned that the criterion agreed upon to measure performance might cause a division to reject a new product, when introduction of the product is in the best interest of the total company.

Tom has asked you to prepare an analysis of these issues. To simplify the analysis, Tom said to use current year's data for Like Magic and Softer together with the projected new product data. You decide to build a spreadsheet model so other acquisitions, capital charges, etc., could be easily analyzed.

C. REQUIREMENTS

1. Review Worksheet 9. A few key financial figures are shown for Like Magic, Softer and the new product. Space is given for you to compute the important components of return on investment and residual income. Residual income should be calculated at the four cost of capital rates shown. You will determine the performance results for the two divisions first without and then with the new product.

The figures presented at the top of Worksheet 9 are based upon valuation of the assets using net book value. In the second section moving down the Worksheet, you are asked to recalculate the return on investment and residual income valuing the assets at gross book value. The lower section of the spreadsheet on Transfer Pricing will be used in assignment 9-B.

2. Retrieve the file **CONTROL**.

3. Enter formulas to compute the Income % of Revenue, Capital Turnover, and Return on Investment for Like Magic and Softer, **cells C7-D9**.

4. Enter formulas to compute the Residual Income at 12%, 14%, 16% and 18% for the two firms in **cells C10-D13**.

5. Total the new product and existing data for Like Magic and Softer in **cells E4-F6**, as if each firm was going to produce the new product. Enter formulas to compute all the figures for return on investment and residual income for the two firms with the new product data included in **cells E7-F13**. Finally, complete the return on investment and residual income figures for just the new product, **cells G7-G13**.

6. Next recalculate return on investment and residual income with plant and equipment valued at gross book value. The formulas to compute return on investment should go into **cells C17-G17**. The formulas to compute residual income at a capital charge of 14% will go into **cells C18-G18**. The figures for operating income in rows 5 are based upon net book value. Depreciation data is given in row 15. The invested capital in row 16 is based upon gross book value.

7. Discuss the performance of Like Magic and Softer using the two criteria of return on investment and residual income. What would be the effect of increasing cost of capital on these criteria of performance? Discuss whether Like Magic or Softer would accept or reject having the new product as part of their division. Discuss the differences in performance between the divisions when gross book value is used versus net book value.

8. What are some alternative definitions of invested capital that might be used by Like Magic and why might they use each one?

9. Discuss the effects on management behavior that can be expected if *economic value added* (EVA) is used to evaluate performance.

10. Print your spreadsheet. Insert your name into the Print Header Line. (See Print Header Line in Chapter 1.)

11. Save your results in the file **CONTROLR**.

OPTIONAL REQUIREMENTS

12. Create two graphs using the electronic spreadsheet and the data you created.

a. Create a column chart comparing *returns on investment* in two sets of five series or data points. Set one will include Like Magic and Softer, with and without the new product, and the new product alone based upon return on investment at net book value. These five series or data points, are in cells **C9-G9**. Set two will include the same five series for Like Magic, Softer and the new product at gross book value. These five series or data points are in cells **C17-G17**. Select "Series in Columns" so the five net book values will appear next to each other. Name the five series, e.g.: 1. *Magic-Alone*, 2. *Softer-Alone*, 3. *Magic+Product*, 4. *Softer+Product*, 5. *New Product*. Enter *Return on Investment* as a title for the chart and *Net and Gross Book Value* as a title for the X axis. (See appendix for help in creating a chart).

b. Create a line graph with five lines of *residual income*, cells **C10-G13**, for Like Magic and Softer with and without the new product. Select series in columns and name the series as described in a above. Enter *Division Residual Income* as a title for the chart and *Cost of Capital 12-18%* as a title for the X axis. (Note: creating an XY – Scatter chart would plot the cost of capital on the X axis, but it is a bit more involved to create than the line chart suggested here. Using the data given, the line and XY charts will look the same because of the even increments for the data used on the X axis, the cost of capital.)

13. Print the graphs.

14. Save your results in the file **CONTROLR.**

D. COMPUTER INFORMATION

1. Name of the file to be retrieved: **CONTROL**
2. Name of the file to save results: **CONTROLR**
3. Cell locations for results: **C4-G18**

E. WORKSHEET 9: Control in Decentralized Organizations

F. CHECK FIGURES

	Figures	Cell Location
ROI, without product, Like Magic:	16.38%	C9
RI, without product, Like Magic @12%:	$1131	C10
ROI, gross book value, Like Magic:	13.73%	C17

LIKE MAGIC COMPANY

Chapter 9-B: Transfer Pricing

A. LEARNING OBJECTIVES

1. Learn the effects and outcomes of basing transfer pricing on market price, variable cost and full cost.
2. Demonstrate the effect on transfer pricing decisions when there is idle capacity versus operating at full capacity.
3. Understand the consequences of rule based transfer pricing and top management involvement.
4. Identify the factors affecting multinational transfer prices.

B. NARRATIVE

Spirit is a firm Like Magic recently purchased. Spirit manufactures the base product for a hydrating cleansing cream that Like Magic plans to produce and sell. Like Magic wants to use a portion of Spirit's output in its new product.

Like Magic has organized their operations so Magic and Spirit are separate divisions under the Like Magic Company. The Magic Division will manufacture the new product. Spirit will manufacture the base product, transferring some of its output to the Magic Division and sell the rest to its current and new customers. Tom Turner, Like Magic's President, decided that the divisions should operate relatively independently from each other. Tom wants each division manager to have significant decision-making authority. He feels this approach will motivate all division managers to operate like they are running their own businesses and thus achieve substantial operating performance. To help achieve this goal, Tom wants to establish a transfer pricing rule that the divisions can use to govern the transfer of Spirit's base product to Magic, for Magic's use in its new cleansing cream.

Tom wants you to prepare an analysis for the divisions and the company using transfer prices that are based upon Spirit's current market price, its variable cost and its full cost. He has asked you to do the analysis for each of two different selling prices for Magic's cream. Tom would like you to show whether the division managers and the company's top management would want the transfer to occur at each price when Spirit has idle production capacity, and when Spirit's production is at full capacity.

C. REQUIREMENTS

1. Review the bottom half of Worksheet 9. The current selling price, variable manufacturing cost and allocated fixed cost is given for Spirit. Similar figures are given for each of two pricing possibilities for Magic, shown as Magic-1 and Magic-2.

    Space is available for you to compute the transfer price and the contribution margin per unit for each division and the total company. At the bottom of

Worksheet 9 is space for you to indicate whether you think management of each division and the total company would say yes, no or be indifferent to the decision to make the transfer of the base cream from Spirit to Magic.

2. Retrieve the file **CONTROLR**.

3. In **row 27,** enter the transfer prices that should be used for transfers at market price, variable cost and full cost. Do this for pricing scenarios Magic-1 and Magic-2.

4. Enter formulas to calculate the contribution margin per unit for the Spirit division in **row 28**, Magic division in **row 31**, and Like Magic company as a whole in **row 34**.

5. Assume Spirit has idle production capacity. Indicate whether each division's management and the company's top management would be in favor of the transfer decision by entering a **Yes, No, or Ind** (for indifference) in rows 36-38. There will be 18 entries in three rows of six columns.

6. Now assume Spirit's production capacity is full with its regular business. Indicate whether each division's management and the company's top management would be in favor of the transfer decision by entering a **Yes, No, or Ind** (for indifference) in rows 41-43.

7. Print your spreadsheet.

8. Save your results in the file **CONTROLR**.

9. Compare and comment on the transfer pricing decisions you indicated in the worksheet. Discuss the issues and problems they raise for Like Magic. What transfer pricing rules do you think that Like Magic should put into practice to govern this type of transfer?

OPTIONAL REQUIREMENTS

Suppose Spirit was producing their base product in a foreign country. Discuss the additional factors that Like Magic should consider in setting a transfer price.

D. COMPUTER INFORMATION

1. Name of the file to be retrieved: **CONTROLR**
2. Name of the file to save results: **CONTROLR**
3. Cell locations for results: **B27-G43**

E. WORKSHEET 9: Control in Decentralized Organizations

Worksheet 9 — Like Magic Company

Profitability Measures	Control in Decentralized Organizations				
	Without Product		**With Product**		**New**
	Magic	**Softer**	**Magic**	**Softer**	**Product**
Sales Revenue	$35,185	$13,870			$4,290
Operating Income	4,230	1,525			600
Invested Capital	25,821	7,575			3,400
Income % of Revenue	------------>				
Capital Turnover	------------>				
Return on Investment	------------>				
}	12%				
Residual Income with}	14%				
Cost of Capital of }	16%				
}	18%				

Comparison: Plant & Equipment at Gross Book Value, Cost of Capital = 14%

Depreciation	$2,164	$540			$306
Invested Capital	30,800	9,975			3,706
Return on Investment	------------>				
Residual Income	14%				

Transfer Pricing	Spirit	Magic-1	Magic-2	800 Units for
Selling Price	$44	$50	$60	Transfer
Variable Manufacturing Cost	16	10	10	
Allocated Fixed Cost	8	4	4	

	* * * * *	Magic-1	* * * * *	* * * * *	Magic-2	* * * * *
	Internal Transfer Pricing			Internal Transfer Pricing		
	Market	Variable	Full	Market	Variable	Full
Spirit Division	Price	Cost	Cost	Price	Cost	Cost
Transfer Price						
Contribution Margin						
Magic Division						
Contribution Margin						
Like Magic Company						
Contribution Margin						

Idle Capacity	Transfer Decision: enter a Yes, No, or Ind for (Indifferent)
Spirit Division	
Magic Division	
Like Magic Company	
Full Capacity	
Spirit Division	
Magic Division	
Like Magic Company	

LIKE MAGIC COMPANY

Chapter 10: Capital Budgeting

A: Discounted Cash Flow and Sensitivity Analysis

A. LEARNING OBJECTIVES

1. Gain understanding of using discounted cash flow as the method of analysis for capital budgeting decisions.
2. Specify the relevant cash flows for an investment project by developing a table of annual figures for alternative decision choices.
3. Learn how to compute the net present value and internal rate of return using an electronic spreadsheet.
4. Prepare an analysis of two competing alternative choices for a capital budgeting project.
5. Determine how the net present value and internal rate of return vary as you vary the cost of capital and the expected value of the cash flows. See how sensitive the capital budgeting decision is to these types of changes.

B. NARRATIVE

Tracy Turner, Executive Vice President of Like Magic, has called a meeting to discuss alternatives for the new computer system Like Magic would like to acquire. She says the company has decided to purchase a new system for order processing, inventory control, production scheduling, and sales forecasting. Like Magic plans to install the new computer system by the end of the year.

You summarize the important factors for the two computer systems being considered. The first choice is to purchase a system to handle the above applications and run the accounting applications currently being processed on a computer system Like Magic owns. With this choice, Like Magic will sell its existing computer. Tracy says the company plans to use this new system for five years, then replace it with advanced equipment. Fidel Fernandez, Director of Purchasing, has obtained purchase quotes for the hardware, software and facilities of $180,000. Fidel estimates this new equipment might be able to be sold for $36,000 after five years, but he has little confidence in that amount. Fidel also obtained a market quote of $15,000 for Like Magic's current computer system. You respond the current computer has a book value of $25,000, and therefore the resale would generate a loss for Like Magic. The company has decided that it will outsource operation of the new system. The quote from the outsourcing firm is $110,000 per year, which should be used as the annual operating costs.

The second choice is to continue to run the accounting applications on the current equipment and buy a smaller computer system to run the new applications. If this choice is made, both the current and the new computer systems would be used for five years and then both would be replaced with an advanced computer system. Fidel estimates the acquisition cost of this new smaller system to be $90,000, and its resale value to be $18,000 after five years, but he also has little confidence in the resale amount. The current computer system will be fully depreciated in two years. The company estimates that outsourcing the operations of both systems will cost $125,000 for each of the next two years and $142,000 for years three through five.

You decide to develop an electronic spreadsheet model on your personal computer to help evaluate this decision. The model will show which choice provides the discounted cash flow that is best over the next five years. This approach will use the net present value and internal rate of return functions that are part of spreadsheet software. You plan to use Like Magic's current cost of capital of 16% as the required rate of return for discounting the future cash inflows and outflows. This rate of return covers costs and risks associated with all of Like Magic's investment capital. (This rate is also called the required rate of return, hurdle, cutoff, or discount rate.) The model will enable you to determine if the best choice of a computer changes as the cost of capital or other estimated values are varied.

C. REQUIREMENTS

1. Review Worksheet 10. The top section lists the critical data inputs and cash flows for the two alternative choices, including the years being effected and the relevant amounts. The last two rows in this top section will hold your calculations of the net present value and internal rate of return. The right four columns, Table of Alternative Estimates, will be used later for sensitivity analysis. The middle section of the Worksheet contains a table for you to complete with the relevant annual cash flows. Fill in some of the cash inflows and outflows in this table.

2. Open the file **CAPBUDGT**.

3. Complete the table of relevant annual cash flows for Choice 1 using the amounts and years given in columns B and C.

a. Create a formula in **cell B21** for the cash outflow for the purchase of the new equipment now. Show cash outflows as negative amounts.

b. Create formulas in **rows 22 and 23** for any appropriate amounts for the resale of the old and the new equipment.

c. Create formulas in the **cells in row 24** to show the annual cash operating costs for each year.

d. Total the cash inflows and outflows for each year in **cells B25-G25.**

4. Complete the table of relevant annual cash flows for Choice 2 in **rows 27-30.**

5. Create formulas for the difference between the cash flows for Choice 1 and Choice 2 in **cells B31-G31**. The figures in these cells show the cash flow advantages or disadvantages by year between the two different decision choices. If you were to sum the figures in these cells, you would get a comparison of the alternatives ignoring the time value of money. This simple comparison disregards the fact that the lower annual costs of Choice 1 comes years after its much larger initial outlay.

6. In **cell C17** create a formula for the net present value of the annual cash inflows and outflows between Choice 1 and Choice 2 using the **NPV (net present value) function**. Use the Cost of Capital in cell **C15** as the **rate** for the net present value and the cash flows for Choice 1-2, in **B31-G31**, as the range of cells for the **value** for the calculation. The following discussion will help you use the NPV function. First select the **Function Wizard** on the Standard Toolbar. Then select **Financial** as the Function Category. Scroll down using the arrow in the right column under **Function Name** to **NPV**. Select **OK**. Enter **C15**, the cost of capital, as the **Rate**. Enter the cash flow now for Choice (1-2), **B31**, as **Value 1**. Enter the cash flows for years 1-5, **C31-G31**, as a range for **Value 2**, or individually for **Values 2-6**. (For a discussion and examples, use *Help* from the menu on the top toolbar, select *Contents and Index,* and enter *net present value,.*)

7. In **cell C16** create a formula for the internal rate of return given the annual cash inflows and outflows between Choice 1 and Choice 2 using the **IRR function**. This command calculates the internal rate of return by a series of approximations from a starting percentage, which is sometimes entered, but often left blank. Use the range of cells for the differences between the annual cash, cells **B31-G31,** as the **Values**. The *Function Wizard and Help* discussed above can be used for **IRR** and *internal rate of return*.

8. Interpret the net present value figure that was calculated? Which choice provides the better financial results for Like Magic? What information does the internal rate of return provide?

9. See how sensitive the decision choice is to other values in the critical data inputs. Each set of values and results will become a column in the Table of Alternative Estimates. To take advantage of the formulas you created, each set of values and the resultant net present value and internal rate of return should be copied to column 1 in the Table.

a. First copy the figures in **C5-C17 to D5-D17**, alternative 1. Use **Copy** and **Paste Special** then **Values** to copy the data. The command *Paste Special - Values* will paste the numerical figures not the formulas into alternative 1.

b. See what happens if the Company uses a cost of capital of 20%. Change **cell C15**, the Cost of Capital, to **20%**. Comment on the change in the net present value. What effect did the change have on the internal rate of return? Why? Would this change suggest a different decision choice? Use **Copy** and **Paste Special** then **Values** to **copy C5-C17 to E5-E17**, to paste the numerical values for this scenario as alternative 2.

c. Now try a pessimistic assumption that the new computer system would have zero resale value at the end of five years. Change **cells C7 and C12**, Resell New Equipment, to **0**. Change the Cost of Capital, **cell 15**, back to the original **16%**. Comment on the change in the net present value. What effect did the changes have on the internal rate of return? Why? Would these changes suggest a different decision choice? Use **Copy** and **Paste Special** then **Values** to **copy C5-C17 to F5-F17**, to create alternative 3.

d. Next examine the results if the company does not have to increase the annual cash operating costs for choice 2 in years 3-5. Change **cell C14** to **125,000**. Change the Resale of the New Equipment cells back to their original values, **change C7 to 36,000 and C12 to 18,000**. Comment on the change in the net present value. What effect did the changes have on the internal rate of return? Why? Would these changes suggest a different decision choice? Again use **Copy** and **Paste Special** then **Values** to **copy C5-C17 to G5-G17**, to create alternative 4.

e. Try other changes that you think might be reasonable possibilities.

10. Print the spreadsheet with your results. Before you print your results, inset your name into the Print Header Line. (See Print Header Line in Chapter 1.)

11. Save your results in the file **CAPBUDGR**.

OPTIONAL REQUIREMENTS

12. Discuss how inflation considerations should be treated in this analysis especially if Like Magic did not get a guaranteed cost in its outsourcing agreement.

D. COMPUTER INFORMATION

1. Name of the file to be retrieved: **CAPBUDGT**
2. Name of the file to save results: **CAPBUDGR**
3. Cell location for results: C5-G17, B21-G31

E. WORKSHEET 10: Capital Budgeting

F. CHECK FIGURES

	Figures	Cell Locations
Cash Flow (Choice 1-2) – Now:	$(75,000)	B31
Net Present Value-original data	$ 9,533	D17

LIKE MAGIC COMPANY

Chapter 10-B: Effects of Income Taxes on Capital Budgeting

A. LEARNING OBJECTIVES

1. Gain understanding of the effect of income taxes on cash inflows, outflows and capital budgeting decisions.
2. Compute the cash savings from income taxes that arise from taking depreciation as an expense on income tax returns.
3. Determine the tax effects and after-tax costs on the relevant data inputs and cash flows in capital budgeting decisions.
4. Prepare an after-tax analysis of two competing alternative choices for a capital budgeting project.

B. NARRATIVE

You want to expand your spreadsheet model for capital budgeting analyses to include the effects of income taxes on the decision. Specifically, you want to determine if including income tax considerations changes the choice between the decision alternatives. You will use Like Magic's marginal income tax rate because it is the tax rate that will affect the additional cash flows generated by the proposed equipment purchase.

A brief review of the United States tax laws governing depreciable assets shows that the current approach is called Modified Accelerated Cost Recovery System (MACRS). Under MACRS, Like Magic's new computer system is classified as 5-year property. Assume the computer equipment is sold but not used in the sixth year so the final year's depreciation is taken.

C. REQUIREMENTS

1. Review the bottom section of Worksheet 10. Note the book value of the old (current) equipment, the current federal income tax rate and an MACRS Depreciation Table for 5-year property. The rows and columns in the table of relevant after-tax cash flows have been expanded over the ones used in part A. They now include lines for the depreciation tax savings, the tax effect on the sale of equipment, and a column for year 6.

2. Open the file you saved **CAPBUDGR**.

3. Copy the original amounts you put in cells **D5-D15** back into **cells C5-C15**.

4. Create two windows by selecting **Windows** then **Split** from the toolbar menu. Scroll in the upper window to see the initial cash flows, and lower windows to see the table to be completed.

5. Complete the relevant after-tax cash inflows and outflows for choice 1 and 2, **cells B39-H53**.

a. Create formulas to compute the after-tax cash flow from the depreciation expense for the new equipment purchase in **rows 40 and 49**. Show the first depreciation tax savings in year 1, assuming the tax savings occurs at the end of the year since the expense occurs throughout the year. (Hint: the formula for each year should include the purchase cost, the appropriate MACRS percentage and the tax rate. You might want to reposition the upper window.) Remember, Like Magic plans to sell but not use this equipment in year 6.

b. Create formulas in **rows 42, 44 and 51** for the income tax effects from the sale of the equipment. Assume the tax effect of the sale of the old equipment occurs in year 1.

6. Create formulas in **row 54** for the difference in after-tax cash flows between choice 1 and choice 2.

7. Complete the net present value of choice 1 versus choice 2 in **cell C17**. Use the Cost of Capital in cell **C15** as the **rate** for the net present value and the cash flows for Choice 1-2, in **B54-H54**, as the range of cells for the **value** for the calculation.

8. Complete the internal rate of return for the after-tax cash flows in **cell C16**.

9. Remove the Windows Split.

10. Change the column title over these latest results to **After Tax, C2-C3**.

11. Print the entire spreadsheet with your results.

12. Save your results in the file **CAPBUDGR**, replacing the file that you previously saved.

13. Discuss how Like Magic should make its decision on the equipment. What qualitative factors should be considered in this decision?

D. COMPUTER INFORMATION

1. Name of the file to be retrieved: **CAPBUDGR**
2. Name of the file to save results: **CAPBUDGR**
3. Cell location for results: B39-H54, C16-C17

E. WORKSHEET 10: Capital Budgeting

F. CHECK FIGURES

	Figures	Cell Locations
Depreciation tax savings, choice 1, year 1:	10,800	C40
After-tax Net Cash Flow - Year 1:	18,900	C54

Worksheet 10 — Like Magic Company

Critical Data Inputs and Cash Flows	Years	Capital Budgeting After Tax	1	Table of Alternative Estimates 2	3	4
CHOICE 1						
Purchase new equipment	Now	$180,000				
Resell old equipment	Now	15,000				
Resell new equipment	5	36,000				
Cash effects of operations	1-5	110,000				
CHOICE 2						
Purchase new equipment	Now	90,000				
Resell new equipment	5	18,000				
Cash effects of operations	1-2	125,000				
Cash effects of operations	3-5	142,000				
Cost of Capital (Rate)		16.0%				
Internal Rate of Return						
Net Present Value						

Relevant Cash Flows	Now	Years Having Cash Flows 1	2	3	4	5
CHOICE 1						
Purchase new equipment						
Resell old equipment						
Resell new equipment						
Cash effects of operations						
Cash Flow - Choice 1						
CHOICE 2						
Purchase new equipment						
Resell new equipment						
Cash effects of operations						
Cash Flow - Choice 2						
Cash Flow (Choice 1-2)						

Worksheet 10 — Like Magic Company

Additional Data for Income Taxes		MACRS Depreciation 5 year property YEAR					
		<u>1</u>	<u>2</u>	<u>3</u>	<u>4</u>	<u>5</u>	<u>6</u>
Book value - old equipment	$25,000						
Income tax rate	30.0%	20.00%	32.00%	19.20%	11.52%	11.52%	5.76%
Relevant After-tax Cash Flows	Now	<u>Years</u> 1	<u>Having</u> 2	<u>Cash</u> 3	<u>Flows</u> 4	5	6
CHOICE 1							
Purchase new equipment							
Depreciation tax savings							
Sale old equipment-Cash							
" " " Tax Effect							
Sale new equipment-Cash							
" " " Tax Effect							
<u>Cash effects of operations</u>							
Cash Flow – Choice 1							
CHOICE 2							
Purchase new equipment							
Depreciation tax savings							
Sale new equipment-Cash							
" " " Tax Effect							
<u>Cash effects of operations</u>							
Cash Flow - Choice 2							
Cash Flow (Choice 1-2)							

LIKE MAGIC COMPANY

Chapter 11: Allocation of Service Department Costs

A: The Direct Method

A. LEARNING OBJECTIVES

1. Learn the principal approaches of allocating costs.
2. Demonstrate the direct method of allocating service department costs to production departments.
3. Show how to allocate the conversion costs of production departments to products.

B. NARRATIVE

Like Magic has recently begun producing and selling a second type of cream for the skin. The company decided to outsource some of the material processing for this new cream until demand is better known. They also decided to put the new cream in an upscale jar that requires more labor in bottling the second cream. These decisions made the material cost somewhat higher for the second cream, reduced the labor content in the processing department, increased labor costs in the bottling department, and enabled Like Magic to save money on capital investment.

Anthony Iococca, Vice President of Manufacturing, is increasingly concerned that the recent increase in manufacturing costs has reduced the profitability of their main cream. Anthony thinks the manufacturing costs of this new cream may be the problem. You suggest Like Magic's cost allocation method might be causing the problem. It has not changed since they were a much smaller one-product company. In addition to adding new products, Like Magic has set up separate service departments to support their manufacturing, these are:

General Support: personnel, building and administration
Computer Support: computer, order processing and scheduling
Factory Support: product management, engineering, quality control, and maintenance
Material Control: receiving, shipping and inventory control

Anthony has asked you to help analyze these costs to determine profitability by product. He especially wants to know the impact of their decisions on both creams. You decide to set up a spreadsheet to compare costs using a few different methods of cost allocation.

C. REQUIREMENTS

1. Review Worksheet 11. The top section lists Like Magic's four service and two production departments with their budgeted conversion costs for the coming year. Also shown are the measures that have been chosen to use as the bases for cost allocation, and the corresponding figures for each department for each allocation base. Space has been provided to allocate the service department costs to the production departments and allocate the cost in the production departments to the two products. In Assignment 11-A you will

use the direct method for allocating the service department costs. The step method will be used in 11-B.

2. Retrieve the file **ALLOCATE**.

3. Using the direct method, enter formulas to compute the cost allocation of the service department conversion costs to the production departments in **cells B18-G23**. Use the measure of output given as the base for allocating each department's costs.

4. Total the departmental costs after allocation in **row 24**.

5. Compute the rates for allocating the production department conversion costs to the products in **row 25**. These rates are expressed as a cost per direct labor hour.

6. Compute the total product cost (material and conversion) per jar for both creams A and B using the rates calculated in #5, putting the results in **cells B38 and B39**.

7. Print your spreadsheet. Before the report is printed, insert your name in the Print Header Line. (See Print Header Line in Chapter 1.)

8. Save your results in the file **ALLOCATR**.

D. COMPUTER INFORMATION

1. Name of the file to be retrieved: **ALLOCATE**
2. Name of the file to save results: **ALLOCATR**
3. Cell location for results: **B18-G25, B38-B39**

E. WORKSHEET 11:   Cost Allocation of Service Departments

F. CHECK FIGURE

	Figures	Cell Locations
Process Dept. total conversion costs after allocation:	$7949	F24
Cost per jar of Cream A:	$19.46	B38

LIKE MAGIC COMPANY

Chapter 11: Allocation of Service Department Costs:

B: The Step Method

A. LEARNING OBJECTIVES

1. Demonstrate the step method of allocating service department costs to production departments.
2. Understand the differences between using departmental and firmwide rates for allocating costs to products.

B. NARRATIVE

You have completed using the direct method of allocating service department conversion costs to the production departments. In this assignment you will use the step method, and then allocate costs in each production department to Like Magic's products. Next you will allocate all of Like Magic's conversion costs to their products using one firmwide rate, their current method of cost allocation

After you have completed the differing methods of cost allocation, you will compare and comment on the advantages and disadvantages of each method of cost allocation. Then you will recommend a cost allocation method for Like Magic to use.

C. REQUIREMENTS

1. Retrieve or continue working with the file **ALLOCATR**.

2. Using the step method, enter formulas to compute the cost allocation of the service department conversion costs to the production departments in **cells B27-G32**. Allocate the conversion costs of the service departments in the sequence given, i.e., General Support first, Computer Support second, etc. Use the measure of output given as the base for allocating each department's costs.

3. Total the departmental conversion costs after allocation in **row 33**.

4. Compute the rates for allocating the production department conversion costs to the products in **row 34**. These rates are expressed as a cost per direct labor hour.

5. Compute the total product cost (material and conversion) per jar for both creams A and B using the rates calculated in #5, putting the results in **cells C38 and C39**.

6. Compute the single firmwide rate for allocating all of Like Magic's conversion costs to their products in **cell G35**. These rates are expressed as a cost per direct labor hour. (Remember to use the costs for all of their departments.)

7. Compute the total product cost (material and conversion) per jar for both creams A and B using the single firmwide rate calculated in #6, putting the results in **cells D38 and D39**.

8. Print your spreadsheet.

9. Save your results in the file **ALLOCATR**.

10. Compare and comment on the potential change for Like Magic from their current firmwide rate to the direct or step method of cost allocation. Discuss the advantages and disadvantages of each choice. Which choice would you recommend for Like Magic?

11. Discuss how these methods of cost allocation could be used to help Like Magic evaluate their initial purchase and manufacturing decisions for their new cream, cream - B.

12. Respond to Anthony Ioccoca's concern that the profitability of their main cream, cream - A, has gone down. Use the figures in your cost allocation for support.

OPTIONAL REQUIREMENTS

13. Discuss the reciprocal method of allocating the conversion costs in the service departments to the production departments.

D. COMPUTER INFORMATION

1. Name of the file to be retrieved: **ALLOCATE**
2. Name of the file to save results: **ALLOCATR**
3. Cell location for results: **B27-G39**

E. WORKSHEET 11: Cost Allocation of Service Departments

F. CHECK FIGURES

	Figures	Cell Location
Cost per jar of Cream A using the firmwide rate:	$20.10	D38

Worksheet 11 — Like Magic Company

Cost Allocation of Service Departments

Service Departments	Measures of Output	Budgeted Conversion Costs	Labor Hours	Computer Entries	People	Liters
General support	People	$1,717	115	2,800	55	
Computer support	Entries	834	51	2,500	24	
Factory support	Labor hours	1,125	72	1,250	34	32
Material control	Liters	812	58	1,600	29	340
Production Departments						
Process	Labor hours	5,084	540	7,200	285	334
Bottling	Labor hours	4,954	284	3,100	148	320

	Cream - A	Cream - B	
Direct material cost	$6.00	$8.00	per jar
Process Dept. labor hours	0.6	0.4	per jar
Bottling Dept. labor hours	0.2	0.7	per jar

Direct Method

	General Support	Computer Support	Factory Support	Material Control	Process	Bottling
Department costs before allocation						
General support						
Computer support						
Factory support						
Material control						
Total costs after allocation						
Production dept. rates:						

Step Method

	General Support	Computer Support	Factory Support	Material Control	Process	Bottling
Department costs before allocation						
General support						
Computer support						
Factory support						
Material control						
Total costs after allocation						
Production dept. rates:						

One firmwide rate:

Total product cost per jar of cream	Direct Method	Step Method	Firmwide rate
Cream - A			
Cream - B			

LIKE MAGIC COMPANY

Chapter 12: Activity-Based Costing

A. LEARNING OBJECTIVES

1. Learn how to implement an activity-based costing system.
2. Demonstrate how to apply activity-based costing in a manufacturing environment.
3. Discuss the differences between activity-based costing and traditional overhead costing using a single overhead cost pool with one cost driver.

B. NARRATIVE

Like Magic is planning to begin producing and selling a third type of cream for the skin. This cream will build upon the success of their recently introduced second cream. The new cream will have more appealing fragrance and creaminess and be sold in an upscale jar. The company found that enhancing their products requires more time and care in manufacturing to meet their high quality standards. This extra time and care is most noticeable in cleaning, set-up, adjusting and testing before and during manufacturing.

Both Tom and Tracy Turner are quite concerned that the right prices be set for their products. Prices are primarily set as a multiple of their manufacturing costs. There must be sufficient increments in prices between their products to help create the perception of value they want in their customers' minds. Tracy thinks that the increasing number of products combined with the increases in complexity of overhead in manufacturing requires a new method of costing. In the past they grouped all their manufacturing overhead costs into a single cost pool which was allocated to products based upon a single cost driver, direct-labor hours. She suggests they implement an activity-based costing system.

After a study, Like Magic determined that the following four activities should be used for overhead if they implement an activity-based costing system:

1. Setup: which includes cleaning to ensure no carry-over of fragrance, color or other characteristics from one cream to the next; special storage and handling of the additive ingredients because of their delicate nature; and adjustments to get just the right amount of each ingredient added.
2. Blending: which requires considerable energy, machine time, supplies, space, etc.
3. Testing: which involves expensive testing equipment, supplies and space for the numerous necessary tests to assure the proper fragrance, feel on the skin and absorbency.
4. Packaging: which is customized by order so they can complete a continuous manufacturing operation.

You have been asked to determine the cost per unit using the proposed activity-based costing system. Then you will compare those costs with what the costs would be using their past traditional costing system. You decide to set up a spreadsheet to complete the analysis.

C. REQUIREMENTS

1. Review Worksheet 12. The top section lists Like Magic's four activities and the cost driver for each activity. For each activity the estimated traceable cost and total physical flow of driver units is given for the coming year. The second section contains several budgeted figures for the coming year for each of their three products. The third section will be used to compute their estimated costs through the cost per unit using activity-based costing. The last section of the worksheet will be used to calculate the cost per unit of their past traditional costing system.

2. Retrieve the file **ACTIVITY**.

3. Following the method in the text, enter formulas to compute the cost per driver unit for each activity in **cells E5-E8.**

4. In the Activity-Based Costing section, enter formulas to compute the overhead cost for each of the four activities for each of the three products in **cells C19-E22**.

5. For each cream, total the overhead costs in **row 23**.

6. Compute the overhead cost per unit for all three creams putting the results in **cells C25-E25**.

7. Insert the direct material and direct labor costs/unit in **cells C26-E27**, then compute the manufacturing cost per unit for each cream in **cells C28-E28** using activity-based costing.

8. In the Traditional Costing section, compute the overhead cost/unit applied using direct-labor hours in **cells C31-E31**. To compute the cost/unit, the estimated traceable overhead costs for all the activities must be grouped into a single cost pool and the single cost driver must include the direct-labor hours for all the products.

9. Insert the direct material and direct labor costs/unit in **cells C32-E33**, then compute the manufacturing cost per unit for each cream in **cells C34-E34** using traditional costing.

10. Print your spreadsheet. Before the report is printed, insert your name in the Print Header Line. (See Print Header Line in Chapter 1.)

11. Save your results in the file **ACTIVITR**.

12. Compare and comment on the potential change for Like Magic from their traditional costing system to the proposed activity-based costing system. Discuss the advantages and disadvantages of each system. Should Like Magic make the change?

13. Discuss the affects each costing system would have on the prices Like Magic sets for its products. Which costing system would be preferable to use to set prices? Provide support for your recommendation.

D. COMPUTER INFORMATION

1. Name of the file to be retrieved: **ACTIVITY**
2. Name of the file to save results: **ACTIVITR**
3. Cell location for results: **E5-E8, C19-E34**

E. WORKSHEET 12: Activity-Based Costing

F. CHECK FIGURE

	Figures	Cell Locations
Setup cost per driver unit:	$242	E5
Cream A total overhead cost:	$2,643,350	C23
Cream B cost per unit:	$23.34	D28

Worksheet 12 **Like Magic Company**

Activity-Based Costing

Activities	Cost Drivers	Estimated Traceable Costs	Total Flow of Driver Units	Cost per Driver Unit
Setup	No. of Setups	$726,000	3,000	
Blending	Machine hours	2,900,000	4,000	
Testing	No. of Tests	1,600,000	16,000	
Packaging	No. of Orders	1,060,000	800	

Budgeted		Cream A	Cream B	Cream C
Units to be produced		650,000	400,000	200,000
Direct-material cost/unit		$6.00	$8.00	$8.40
Direct-labor cost/unit		$7.20	$9.90	$10.80
Number of Setups		1,300	1,000	700
Number of Machine hours		1,700	1,400	900
Number of Tests		5,000	6,000	5,000
Number of Orders		450	240	110
Number of Labor hours		520,000	440,000	240,000

Estimated Costs			
Setup			
Blending			
Testing			
Packaging			
Total Overhead			

Activity-Based Costing			
Overhead cost/unit			
Direct-material cost/unit			
Direct-labor cost/unit			
Cost per unit			

Traditional Costing			
Overhead cost/direct labor hour			
Overhead cost/unit			
Direct-material cost/unit			
Direct-labor cost/unit			
Cost per unit			

LIKE MAGIC COMPANY

Chapter 13: Overhead Application

A: Applying Factory Overhead

A. LEARNING OBJECTIVES

1. Understand the logic and methods for computing budgeted factory overhead rates.
2. Learn how to compute applied factory overhead.
3. Demonstrate how overapplied and underapplied factory overhead are determined.
4. Learn to compare and select the best cost drivers for overhead application.

B. NARRATIVE

Like Magic has expanded the number and mix of products it manufactures and sells. After producing the basic compound, material is added to meet varying skin textures and fragrances desired. Packaging now ranges from simple to upscale containers. Like Magic has begun to produce and sell some of its products as private label brands for a few exclusive retail store chains.

This increase in products has led management to seek more timely and improved information on product costs. As the new controller, you decide to provide this information by applying factory overhead to products. Overhead will be applied using a budgeted or predetermined factory overhead rate. First you need to evaluate alternative activity bases for calculating overhead rates and applying overhead. The goal is to ensure a strong cause-and-effect relationship between variations in actual factory overhead and the base selected. You decide to prepare a comparative analysis of several budgeted overhead rates on applied overhead and gross profit. Annual budgeted figures will be used to calculate the budgeted overhead rates. Using annual data will avoid month-to-month fluctuations in production volume, related activities, and overhead costs.

Since you have increased your confidence in the use of electronic spreadsheets and computer modeling, you have decided to use an electronic spreadsheet for this overhead analysis.

C. REQUIREMENTS

1. Review Worksheet 13. The top section is the Budgeted Factory Overhead Application Table. It contains five possible activity bases for applying overhead, budgeted data that Like Magic developed prior to the start of the year, the actual results that Like Magic incurred during the year, and the columns which you will complete for this assignment. The remainder of Worksheet 13 will be used in part B of this chapter.

2. Open the file **OVERHEAD.**

3. Enter formulas in **cells D6-D10**, to calculate the Budgeted Overhead Rates for the five activity rate bases: direct labor expenses, direct labor hours, machine hours, pounds of material, and production in units.

4. Enter formulas in **cells E6-E10**, to compute the Overhead Applied for each of the five activity rate bases.

5. Compute the Underapplied or Overapplied Overhead, **cells F6-F10**, for each of the five activity rate bases.

6. Print the Budgeted Manufacturing Overhead Application Table. Before you print your report, insert your name into the Print Header Line. (See Print Header Line in Chapter 1.)

7. Save your results in file **OVERHEDR**.

8. Interpret the results in the table. What is the meaning of an underapplied balance versus an overapplied balance? Why would overhead be underapplied using some of the activity bases and overapplied using other bases? Are there any activity bases which should not be considered for possible use and if not, why? Which base or bases would you recommend? Would your recommendation change if Like Magic was planning significant automation during the next year?

D. COMPUTER INFORMATION

1. Name of the file to be retrieved: **OVERHEAD**
2. Name of the file to save results: **OVERHEDR**
3. Cell locations for results: **D6-F10**

E. WORKSHEET 13: Budgeted Factory Overhead Application Table and Year-end Disposition - Under (Over) Applied Overhead.

F. CHECK FIGURES

Activity base	Figures	Cell Location
Labor Expenses:	($ 335)	F6
Pounds of Material:	(1060)	F9

LIKE MAGIC COMPANY

Chapter 13-B: Accounting at the End of the Year

A. LEARNING OBJECTIVES

1. Understand how the Cost of Goods Manufactured, Cost of Goods Sold and Income Statement are affected by using applied factory overhead.
2. Learn how to dispose of underapplied and overapplied overhead at the end of the year.
3. Demonstrate the method of immediate or direct write-off of underapplied and overapplied overhead.
4. Learn how to prorate the year-end differences between actual and applied manufacturing overhead among Cost of Goods Sold, Work-in-Process Inventory and Finished Goods Inventory.

B. Narrative

Before implementing a budgeted factory overhead rate, you would like to see how gross profit for Like Magic would have been affected by using applied rather than actual overhead for the five activity bases. You also want to create a model of the financial schedules and statements using applied overhead based on a budgeted overhead rate.

Using applied factory overhead will usually leave an underapplied or overapplied overhead amount at the end of the year. You would like to show the effect of the end of the year accounting on gross profit if the underapplied or overapplied overhead amount is written off to cost of goods sold. Sometimes the underapplied or overapplied overhead would be large at the end of the year, say greater than 10% of the total amount incurred. If Like Magic used pounds of material as the rate base for budgeted overhead rate, overapplied overhead would be greater than 10% above actual factory overhead expenses. You want to compare the effect of writing this overapplied amount off to cost of goods sold versus prorating it among cost of goods sold and the appropriate inventory accounts.

C. REQUIREMENTS

1. Review Worksheet 13 again. In the second section of the Worksheet, YEAR-END DISPOSITION – UNDER (OVER) APPLIED OVERHEAD, there are two columns for gross profit for the five activity bases. The gross profits before write-off are given. You will complete the gross profits after write-off. Following the Additional Data, schedules are given for Cost of Goods Manufactured and Cost of Goods Sold. These schedules should be completed with overhead applied using pounds of material as the base in determining the overhead rate. The Underapplied/Overapplied Overhead This Year section of the Worksheet provides space for you to prorate and directly write off the underapplied or overapplied overhead among the inventory accounts and cost of goods sold. Finally, the short Income Statement should be completed.

2. Retrieve or continue using file **OVERHEDR**.

3. Calculate the **Gross Profit After Write-Off for the five activity bases, cells E14-E18**, so that all of the underapplied or overapplied manufacturing overhead is charged to Cost of Goods Sold at yearend. What do you observe about gross profit for the activity bases? Explain the reason for these results in gross profit for the activity bases.

4. Overapplied overhead using pounds of material as the activity base was quite large at the end of the year. Enter formulas to complete the **Cost of Goods Manufactured** and **Cost of Goods Sold** for **Normal Costing for this year using Pounds of Material for an Overhead Base, cells B26-B38**.

5. Continuing to use pounds of material as the overhead rate base, compare the year-end closing by writing the overapplied overhead off to cost of goods sold with prorating it among cost of goods sold and the inventory accounts. Complete the year-end disposition, **Underapplied/Overapplied Overhead This Year,** using pounds of material as the activity rate base, **cells B43-E46**.

a. Complete the **Year-end Unadjusted Balance** for the three accounts: WIP Inventory, Finished Goods Inventory and Cost of Goods Sold, **cells B43-B45**. Calculate a total of the three accounts in **cell B46**.

b. Prorate the **Overapplied Overhead, cell F9**, among the three accounts: WIP Inventory, Finished Goods Inventory, and Cost of Goods Sold, putting the formulas for the proration in **cells C43-C45**. Total the proration in **cell C46** and visually check that this total equals the overapplied overhead in cell F9.

c. Complete and total the **Proration: Year-end Adjusted Balance** for the three accounts, **cells D43-D46**.

d. Enter formulas in **cells E43-E45**, to complete the **Direct Write-off: Year-end Adjusted Balance** for the three accounts by closing the overapplied overhead to cost of goods sold. Total the direct write-off in **cell E46**.

6. Using pounds of material as the overhead rate base, enter formulas to complete the Income Statement for Proration, **cells D48-D50,** and Direct Write-off, **cells E48-E50**.

7. Print your results.

8. Save your results in file **OVERHEDR**.

9. Note the differences between direct write-off and proration on the year-end value of cost of goods sold, finished goods inventory and work in process inventory. Are these differences large? Why is gross profit different when the write-off method is used than when the proration method is used? If Like Magic wrote this overapplied overhead off to cost of goods sold, would their statements be misleading?

D. COMPUTER INFORMATION

1. Name of the file to be retrieved: **OVERHEDR**
2. Name of the file to save results: **OVERHEDR**
3. Cell locations for results: **B26-E50**

E. WORKSHEET 13: Budgeted Manufacturing Overhead Application Table and Year-end Disposition - Under (Over) Applied Overhead

F. CHECK FIGURES

Account	Year-end Proration	Adjusted Balance Write-off
Adjusted Cost of Goods Sold	$21,945	$21,820

Worksheet 13 — Like Magic Company

BUDGETED FACTORY OVERHEAD APPLICATION TABLE

Factory Overhead and Bases	Budget	Actual	Budgeted Overhead Rate	Factory Overhead Applied	Under (Over) Applied
Factory overhead expenses	$6,286	$6,477	xxxxxx	xxxxxx	xxxxxx
Direct labor expenses	$8,240	$8,929			
Direct labor hours	824	840			
Machine hours	515	547			
Pounds of material	206	247			
Production in units	1,030	1,100			

YEAR-END DISPOSITION - UNDER (OVER) APPLIED OVERHEAD

Immediate (Direct) Write-off

Factory Overhead Bases	Gross Profit Before Write-Off	Gross Profit After Write-Off
Direct labor expenses	$13,030	
Direct labor hours	13,434	
Machine hours	13,165	
Pounds of material	12,305	
Production in units	13,129	

Additional Data

ACCOUNTS	Last Year-end	This Year-end	ACCOUNTS	This Year
Direct material inventory	$700	$840	Sales	$35,185
Work in process inventory	1,400	1,710	Direct material used	7,024
Finished goods inventory	1,050	1,350	Direct labor	8,929

Normal Costing Using Pounds of Material for an Overhead Base

Cost of Goods Manufactured
- Work in process beginning inventory
- Direct material used
- Direct labor
- Factory overhead applied
- Total
- Work in process ending inventory
- Cost of goods manufactured

Cost of Goods Sold (unadjusted)
- Finished goods beginning inventory
- Cost of goods manufactured
- Cost of goods available
- Finished goods ending inventory
- Cost of goods sold (unadjusted)

Underapplied/Overapplied Overhead This Year

Pounds of Material as Overhead Rate Base	Year-end Unadjusted Balance	Proration	Proration Year-end Adjusted Balance	Direct Write-off Year-end Adjusted Balance
Work in process inventory				
Finished goods inventory				
Cost of goods sold				
Total ------->				

Income Statement

	Proration	Direct Write-off
Sales		
Adjusted cost of goods sold		
Gross profit		

81

LIKE MAGIC COMPANY

Chapter 14: Process Costing Systems

A: The Initial Department

A. LEARNING OBJECTIVES

1. Understand the nature of continuous production operations and why process costing is used.
2. Learn to calculate output in terms of equivalent units of production.
3. Demonstrate the principal differences between the weighted-average and the first-in, first-out (FIFO) methods for product costing.
4. Show how to prepare production cost reports using both the weighted-average and FIFO methods for product costing.

B. NARRATIVE

Like Magic manufactures their creams in a continuous production operation. Because they are continuing to seek improved methods for applying costs to their products, you have decided to use a processing costing system. All products go through three departments: blending, finishing and packaging. In part A of this chapter, you will apply costs to products for blending, the first manufacturing department. Part B of this chapter requires costs to be applied for finishing, a subsequent manufacturing department. (Part B can be solved without doing part A.)

Blending starts by combining eighty percent of the direct materials used in this department to form the basic compound for their cream. Near the end of processing in this department, the additional twenty percent of the direct materials are added. Labor and overhead are added evenly throughout this department. After completion in the blending department, the in-process compound is moved to the finishing department. In finishing, materials are added to produce products with varying skin texture and fragrance characteristics. After finishing, the completed cream compounds are moved to the packaging department. In packaging, jars are filled with the creams, boxed, and the boxes are put into cartons. The filled cartons are then sealed and moved to finished goods inventory.

You are selecting between the weighted-average and first-in, first-out (FIFO) methods for process costing. You have decided to prepare a comparison for Quarter 1, showing: equivalent units, cost per equivalent unit, and a production cost report for both methods. Your reports will be developed using an electronic spreadsheet to permit easy variation for differing conditions.

You were pleased with the results of using applied overhead, so you will use normalized costs for process costing. Normalized manufacturing costs consist of actual direct material, actual direct labor and applied overhead (using a predetermined overhead rate.) The normalized costs have already been calculated.

C. REQUIREMENTS

Note: Solutions can be completed for either or both the weighted-average or FIFO methods. The discussion below is for solution by both methods.

1. Review Worksheet 14. Page 1 is used for part A, and pages 2 and 3 for part B. The data in the top section contains the flow of physical units and the percentage completed for material and conversion of beginning and ending inventories. Next, the costs in beginning inventory and costs added are shown. The remaining sections on page one are to be completed for part A. First, equivalent units will be calculated for the weighted-average and the FIFO methods of process costing. Then the weighted-average method should be used to compute the cost per equivalent unit and application of costs. Next, the FIFO method should be used to compute the cost per equivalent unit and application of costs. Finally, there is a check or second method of cost assignment for the FIFO method.

2. Retrieve the file **PROCESS**.

3. Complete the **Flow of Production** section by entering formulas in **cells B13-D22**. Insert formulas for the physical units in **B13-B18**. Then calculate the equivalent unit components in rows **16-17**. Next, total these equivalent unit components to determine the equivalent units for the current period for the weighted-average method, **C19** and **D19**. Determine the equivalent units of work from prior period in beginning inventory, **cells C21** and **D21**. Lastly, determine the equivalent units for the current period using the FIFO method, **C22** and **D22**.

4. Complete the **Weighted-Average Method, Costs to Account For, cells B25-D27**. Take the dollar amounts from the process costing data, cells C9-D10. Using these costs and the equivalent units you calculated in #3, compute the unit costs, weighted-average, **cells B28-D28**.

5. Complete the **Applications of costs, Weighted-Average Method, cells B31-D36**. Use the equivalent units and costs per equivalent unit that you calculated in #3 and #4.

6. Complete the **FIFO Method, Costs to Account For, B39-D41**. Take the dollar amounts from the process costing data, cells C9-D10. Using these costs and the equivalent units you calculated in #3, compute the unit costs, FIFO, **cells B42-D42**.

7. Complete the **Applications of costs, FIFO Method, cells B46-D50**. Use the equivalent units and costs per equivalent unit that you calculated in #3 and #6.

8. Complete the **Check: Total Costs of Work Completed and Transferred Out, FIFO Method, cells B52-B57**. Use the equivalent units that you calculated.

9. Save your results in the file **PROCESSR**.

10. Print your results. Before you print your report, insert your name into the Print Header Line. (See Print Header Line in Chapter 1.)

11. Note that the Total Costs Accounted For are the same for the weighted-average and the FIFO methods.

D. COMPUTER INFORMATION

1. Name of the file to be retrieved: **PROCESS**
2. Name of the file to save results: **PROCESSR**
3. Cell locations for results: **B13-D57**

E. WORKSHEETS 14: Process Costing

F. CHECK FIGURES

	Weighted-Avg.	FIFO
Equivalent Units of Material	312	248
Cost/Equivalent Unit of Material	$ 4.42	$ 4.15
Total Cost Completed and Transferred Out	$3134	$3182

LIKE MAGIC COMPANY

Chapter 14-B: Process Costing - Subsequent Department

(Part B can be solved without having done part A.)

A. LEARNING OBJECTIVES

1. Understand how transferred-in units and costs from a prior department affect process costing.
2. Demonstrate how to calculate equivalent units and prepare production cost reports, using both the weighted-average and FIFO methods for product costing, for a department which has transferred-in units and costs.

B. NARRATIVE

Like Magic's finishing department has the basic compound for their cream transferred in after it has been prepared in their blending department. In finishing, materials are added to produce products with varying skin texture and fragrance characteristics. All direct materials are added at the start of finishing. Conversion costs are added evenly throughout the finishing department. After finishing, the completed cream compounds are moved to the packaging department.

Before deciding between the weighted-average and first-in, first-out (FIFO) methods for process costing, you decide to prepare a comparison for Quarter 1 for the finishing department. The report will show: equivalent units, cost per equivalent unit, and a production cost report for both methods. These reports will also be developed using an electronic spreadsheet to permit easy variation for differing conditions. You will continue to use normalized costs for process costing. Normalized manufacturing costs consist of actual direct material, actual direct labor and applied overhead (using a predetermined overhead rate.) The normalized costs have already been calculated. For simplicity, transferred-in units and costs have been supplied and do not have to be taken from part A.

C. REQUIREMENTS

Note: Solutions can be completed for either or both the weighted-average or FIFO methods. The discussion below is for solution by both methods.

1. Review Worksheet 14. Page 1 is used for part A and pages 2 and 3 for part B. See the discussion in part A, #1, for a discussion of the worksheet.

2. Retrieve or continue to use the file **PROCESSR**.

3. Complete the **Flow of Production** section by entering formulas in **cells B69-E75**. Insert formulas for the physical units in **B69-B74**. Then calculate the equivalent unit components in **rows 72-73**. Next, total these equivalent unit components to determine the equivalent units for the current period for the weighted-average method, **C75-E75**. Determine the

equivalent units of work from prior period in beginning inventory, **cells C77-E77**. Lastly, determine the equivalent units for the current period using the FIFO method, **C78-E78**.

4. Complete the **Weighted-Average Method, Costs to Account For, cells B81-E83**. Take the dollar amounts from the process costing data, cells C65-E66. Using these costs and the equivalent units you calculated in #3, compute the unit costs, weighted-average, **cells B84-E84**.

5. Complete the **Applications of costs, Weighted-Average Method, cells B86-D92**. Use the equivalent units and costs per equivalent unit that you calculated in #3 and #4.

6. Complete the **FIFO Method Costs to Account For, B95-E97**. Take the dollar amounts from the process costing data, cells C65-E66. Using these costs and the equivalent units you calculated in #3, compute the unit costs, FIFO, **cells B98-E98**.

7. Complete the **Applications of costs, FIFO Method, cells B101-D106**. Use the equivalent units and costs per equivalent unit that you calculated in #3 and #6.

8. Complete the **Check: Total Costs of Work Completed and Transferred Out, FIFO Method, cells B108-B113**. Use the equivalent units that you calculated.

9. Save your results in the file **PROCESSR**.

10. Print your results.

11. Note that the Total Costs Accounted For are the same for the weighted-average and the FIFO methods. (The same dollar cost transferred-in is assumed for both methods.)

D. COMPUTER INFORMATION

Name of the file to be retrieved: **PROCESS**
Name of the file to save results: **PROCESSR**
Cell locations for results: **B69-F113**

E. WORKSHEETS 14: Process Costing

F. CHECK FIGURES

	Weighted-Avg.	FIFO
Equivalent Units Transferred-in	340	240
Cost/Equivalent Unit of Material	$ 1.12	$ 1.13
Total Cost Complete and Transferred Out	$4792	$4786

LIKE MAGIC COMPANY

Chapter 14-C: Standard Costs in Process Costing

A. LEARNING OBJECTIVES

1. Understand why standard costs simplify the calculation of product costs for continuous production operations.
2. Learn why standard costs eliminate the conflicts between weighted-average and FIFO methods for product costing.
3. Demonstrate how to assign costs to products using standard costs in process costing.

B. NARRATIVE

Like Magic is still having a hard time choosing between the weighted-average and FIFO methods for product costing. You have just come back from a seminar on standard costs for product costing in industries like yours. You decide to try calculating your product costs for Quarter 1 for the blending department. Because of efficiency you decide to continue using the spreadsheet for this assignment.

C. REQUIREMENTS

1. Review the last section on page 3 of Worksheet 14. This section contains the standard costs for process costing and a table for you to assign costs using the standard costs.

2. Retrieve or continue working with the file **PROCESSR**.

3. Reposition the spreadsheet so rows 116-125 are on the screen. Cells B116-D116 contain the standard costs for the blending department.

4. Enter formulas to complete the **Application of Costs, Standard Cost in Process Costing, B120-D125**. Use the equivalent units you calculated in part A for the blending department under the FIFO method. Both the standard cost and the FIFO methods use "work done during the current period only" for calculating equivalent units.

5. Save your results again in the file **PROCESSR**.

6. Print your results.

7. Why doesn't the total cost accounted for using standard costs equal the total costs to account for?

D. COMPUTER INFORMATION

Name of the file to be retrieved: **PROCESSR**
Name of the file to save results: **PROCESSR**
Cell location for results: **B120-D125**

E. WORKSHEET 14: Process Costing

F. CHECK FIGURES

Total costs accounted for   **$3881**

Worksheet 14 — Like Magic Company

PROCESS COSTING

BLENDING DEPARTMENT — Quarter 1

	Units	Material	Conversion
Beginning inventory	80	80%	50% completed
Started during month	250		
Completed during month	240		
Ending inventory	90	80%	50% completed

Costs	Material	Conversion
Beginning inventory	$350	$500
Costs added in current month	1,030	1,961

Flow of Production

Work in Process	Physical Units	Equivalent Units Material	Conversion
Beginning inventory			
Started during month			
To account for			
Completed and transferred out			
Ending Inventory			
Units accounted for			
Equivalent units, weighted average	------------>		
Less: equivalent units of work from prior period in beginning inventory			
Equivalent units, FIFO	------------>		

Weighted-Average Method

Costs to Account For	Total Costs	Direct Material Costs	Conversion
Beginning inventory			
Costs added currently			
Total costs to account for			
Unit costs, weighted-average			

Application of Costs	Total Costs	Equivalent Units	Cost per Equivalent Unit
Completed and transferred out			
Ending Inventory			
Direct materials			
Conversion costs			
Total ending inventory			
Total costs accounted for			

FIFO Method

Costs to Account For	Total Costs	Direct Material	Conversion Costs
Beginning Inventory			
Costs added currently			
Total costs to account for			
Unit costs, FIFO			

Application of Costs	Total Costs	Equivalent Units	Cost per Equivalent Unit
Ending Inventory			
Direct materials			
Conversion costs			
Total ending inventory			
Completed and transferred out			
Total costs accounted for			

Check: Total Costs of Work Completed and Transferred Out

- Beginning inventory
- Additional costs to complete
  - Direct materials
  - Conversion costs
- Started and completed
- Total costs transferred out

Worksheet 14 — Like Magic Company

FINISHING DEPARTMENT	Quarter 1			
	Units		Material	Conversion
Beginning inventory	100		100%	50% completed
Transferred in	240			
Completed during month	260			
Ending inventory	80		100%	50% completed
Costs		Transferred in	Material	Conversion
Beginning inventory		$1,300	$110	$190
Costs added in current month		$3,134	$272	$1,090

Flow of Production Work in Process	Physical Units	Transferred in Units	Equivalent Units Material	Conversion
Beginning inventory				
Started during month				
To account for				
Completed and transferred out				
Ending Inventory				
Units accounted for				
Equivalent units, weighted average	------------>			
Less: equivalent units of work from prior period in beginning inventory				
Equivalent units, FIFO	------------>			

Weighted-Average Method Costs to Account For	Total Costs	Transferred In	Direct Material	Conversion Costs
Beginning inventory				
Costs added currently				
Total costs to account for				
Unit costs, weighted-average				

Application of Costs	Total	Equivalent units	Cost per equivalent Unit	
Completed and transferred out				
Ending Inventory				
Transferred in				
Direct materials				
Conversion costs				
Total ending inventory				
Total costs accounted for				

FIFO Method Costs to Account For	Total Costs	Transferred In	Direct Material	Conversion Costs
Beginning Inventory				
Costs added currently				
Total costs to account for				
Unit costs, FIFO				

Application of Costs	Total	Equivalent units	Cost per equivalent Unit	
Ending Inventory				
Transferred in				
Direct materials				
Conversion costs				
Total ending inventory				
Completed and transferred out				
Total costs accounted for				

Check: Total Costs of Work Completed and Transferred Out
Beginning inventory
Additional costs to complete
Direct materials
Conversion costs
Started and completed
Total costs transferred out

Worksheet 14   Like Magic Company

Standard Costs in Process Costing - Blending Department Quarter 1			
	Total	Material	Conversion
Standard Cost per Unit		$4.40	$8.80
Application of Costs	Total Costs	Equivalent Units	Cost per Equivalent Unit
Completed and transferred out			
Ending Inventory			
Direct materials			
Conversion costs			
Total ending inventory			
Total costs accounted for			

LIKE MAGIC COMPANY

Chapter 15: The Statement of Cash Flows

A: The Direct Method

A. LEARNING OBJECTIVES

1. Understand the net cash flow in an enterprise and how it differs from net income.
2. Learn the composition of the statement of cash flow.
3. Demonstrate how to compute the major cash flows in an enterprise using the direct method.
4. Use an electronic spreadsheet to build a model linking a company's income statement and balance sheet to its statement of cash flows.

B. NARRATIVE

Like Magic has experienced considerable growth since it started in business. They expect significant additional increases in volume over the next few years. These increases will require sizable additions of people, material, plant and equipment. As controller, you are concerned about the impact of this growth on cash flow. You know that many young expanding firms run short of cash and raising cash on short notice is not easy to do. Therefore, you have decided to do some cash planning.

You have retrieved printed copies of Like Magic's income statement and balance sheet for the year that just ended. These are displayed in Worksheet 15. Note that the comparative balance sheet contains a column to indicate the increases or decreases from last yearend to this yearend. Worksheet 15 also includes additional data extracted from the general ledger, which will be needed to construct the statement of cash flows.

You are pleased with your accounting model, which takes information from your general ledger and generates the income statement, balance sheet and supporting schedules. You would like to extend your model to automatically produce your statement of cash flows. This approach will:

1. Logically tie the statement of cash flows to the general ledger, balance sheet and income statement.

2. Produce the statement of cash flows without the need to make additional entries.

3. Ease and speed changes to data and asking "what-if" types of questions, with the results being seen moments after the data has been entered.

C. REQUIREMENTS (The Direct Method of Reporting Cash Flows from Operations)

1. Review Worksheet 15. In the Comparative Balance Sheet, compute the increases or decreases between the yearends for some of the accounts to observe the changes. These changes in the balance sheet accounts will be used to help prepare the Statement of Cash Flows. Examine the Statement of Cash Flows to determine where the data will be obtained to complete the statement. The source of the data will be the income statement, the balance sheet and the additional data from the general ledger.

2. Use Excel to open the file **CASHFLOW**. This file contains all of the data that you will need, displayed in the Income Statement, Balance Sheet and additional data from the General Ledger. It also includes the Statement of Cash Flows to be completed.

3. For each account in the **Comparative Balance Sheet**, enter formulas in **cells D18-D46** to calculate the increases or decreases between the yearend amounts. You should be able the copy the first formula to all of the lines in the Comparative Balance Sheet where increases or decreases must be calculated.

4. Complete the **Statement of Cash Flows**. Each entry in this statement should be a formula using the cell locations from the income statement, balance sheet or additional data from the general ledger. For example, in **cell C55**, the formula for Sales Revenue in the Statement of Cash Flows would be +C2, the cell in the Income Statement containing Sales Revenue. The following will help you complete the Statement of Cash Flows.

a. Reposition the screen so that row 1 is the top row. Move the cell pointer to row 11 and split the screen into two windows by selecting **Windows** from the menu at the top of the screen, then selecting **Split** from the drop-down menu. The income statement will be in the upper window. Display the top of the Statement of Cash Flows in the lower window by moving down in the lower window.

b. Next, move the cell pointer to **C55** and enter the **Sales Revenue** as a formula. Remember if you want a number that is in one cell to appear in a second cell, in the second cell enter a + and the first cell's location. The Sales Revenue figure in the Income Statement will automatically be transferred to the Sales Revenue figure in the Statement of Cash Flows.

c. Move down in the upper window until the Accounts Receivable figures in the Balance Sheet appear in the upper window. Go to the **Change in Accounts Receivable** in the Statement of Cash Flows. Insert a formula in **cell C56** for the change in accounts receivable. (Remember increases in accounts receivable must be deducted from sales to determine the amount of cash received from customers.)

d. Create a formula for the **Cash Received from Customers** in **cell D57**. The major classes of cash flow are put into column D, and the supporting data into column C.

e. Complete the Statement of Cash Flows. The data for the sections on Cash Flows from Investing Activities and from Financing Activities can be taken from the table of **Additional data from the General Ledger**. Some of the lines under these two latter sections will not have any dollar amounts for this assignment. Pay close attention to whether each entry should be positive or negative. After completing the statement, clear the split windows by selecting **Windows** then **Remove Split** from the menu at the top of the screen.

5. Print your Statement of Cash Flows. Before printing your report, insert your name in the Print Header Line. (See Print Header Line in Chapter 1.)

6. Save your results in file **CASHFLWS**.

7. Where could you have obtained the figures for Purchase of Long Term Investment, Proceeds from the Sale of Bonds, and the Principle Payment of the Long-term Debt, if they were not included in the table of Additional data from the General Ledger?

8. Discuss whether the dividends figures used to calculate retained earnings should be used as the dividends paid for the Statement of Cash Flows?

D. COMPUTER INFORMATION

1. Name of the file to be retrieved: **CASHFLOW**
2. Name of the file to save results: **CASHFLWS**
4. Cell locations for results: **D18-D46, C55-D88**

E. WORKSHEET 15 - Statement of Cash Flows

F. CHECK FIGURES

	Amount	Cell Location
Cash Received from Customers:	$33,901	D57
Cash Payments to Suppliers and Employees:	28,793	D70
Net Cash Provided by Operating Activity:	3,568	D74
Net Increase (Decrease) in Cash:	1,468	D86

LIKE MAGIC COMPANY

Chapter 15-B: The Indirect Method

A. LEARNING OBJECTIVES

1. Demonstrate how to compute the major cash flows in an enterprise using the indirect method.
2. Reconcile net income and net cash flows provided by operating activity.

B. NARRATIVE

You conclude the Statement of Cash Flows provides useful information on the sources of the increases and decreases in cash during the last year. The direct method for the statement preparation clearly shows the actual classes of cash receipts and payments during the period.

Like Magic's CPA firm advises you to provide a separate schedule reconciling net income and net cash flow from your operating activities for the year. Your accounting firm says this reconciliation, also called the indirect method, will provide a useful link to the income statement and balance sheet.

You decide to add this schedule for reconciling net income and net cash from operating activities to your electronic spreadsheet of the Statement of Cash Flows. Then you will assess the benefits provided by the direct versus the indirect method of cash flow statement preparation.

C. REQUIREMENTS

1. Retrieve or continue using the file **CASHFLWS**.

2. Split the screen into two windows with the window across the middle of the screen. Position the net income row in the income statement in the upper window of your screen and the Reconciliation of Net Income and Net Cash Flow from Operating Activities, row 90, in the lower window.

3. Complete the schedule for the reconciliation, **cells C90-D102**.

4. Compare the **Net Cash Provided by Operating Activities** that you just calculated in **cell D102**, with the Net Cash Provided by Operating Activities in **cell D74** that you calculated in part A. They should be equal.

5. Print your Reconciliation of Net Income and Net Cash Flow from Operating Activities.

6. Save your results in file **CASHFLWS**.

D. COMPUTER INFORMATION

1. Name of the file to be retrieved: **CASHFLWS**
2. Name of the file to save results: **CASHFLWS**
3. Cell locations for results: **C90-D102**

E. WORKSHEET 15 - Statement of Cash Flows and Reconciliation of Net Income and Net Cash Flow from Operating Activities

LIKE MAGIC

Chapter 15-C: Additional Cash Flows

A. LEARNING OBJECTIVES

1. Demonstrate how an electronic spreadsheet containing a statement of cash flows can be modified to include additional cash receipts and payments.
2. See how using formulas in an electronic spreadsheet speed up making revisions.

B. NARRATIVE

As you review your automated accounting model, you think back to December when Anthony Iococca, Like Magic's Vice President of Manufacturing, burst into your office. He had just heard about a new automated processing machine with significantly higher capacity, greater throughput and increased efficiency than your current machine. It cost $3,000,000, and he wanted to purchase one to replace the current machine. You thought that purchase would not leave sufficient current cash for the firm to cover other budgeted items. To see about raising additional cash you called Rodney Rukeyser for investment financing. Rodney thought his group could sell another 50,000 shares of your common stock at the current market price of $18 per share.

You wonder how your new electronic spreadsheet model could have been used to simulate the effects of these proposed changes. To help plan for future financing and investing, you decide to revise your Statement of Cash Flow as if the above activities had taken place near the very end of the year. If Like Magic had gone ahead, the following actions would have been the most likely to occur:

1. Equipment costing $3,000,000 would be purchased for $2,000,000 in cash and an increase in long-term debt of $1,000,000.

2. Current equipment that cost $200,000 new, and on which there was accumulated depreciation of $80,000, would be sold for its book value.

3. 50,000 shares of common stock would be issued at $18 per share.

C. REQUIREMENTS

1. Retrieve or continue using file **CASHFLWS**.

2. Change the amounts in the Statement of Cash Flows to include the activities discussed above. Go to the Statement of Cash Flow cells and enter any new or changed data or.

3. Print your revised Statement of Cash Flow.

4. Save this revised spreadsheet under a new file name, e.g., **CASHFLWX**.

D. COMPUTER INFORMATION

1. Name of the file to be retrieved: **CASHFLWS**
2. Name of the file to save results: **CASHFLWX**
3. Cell locations for results: **D18-D46, C55-D88**

E. CHECK FIGURES

	Amount	**Cell Location**
Cash: this year-end:	$1003	D88

Worksheet 15 — Like Magic Company

LIKE MAGIC: Income Statement

Sales Revenue		$35,185
Cost of Goods Sold		21,820
Gross Profit		13,365
Marketing Expenses	7,228	
General and Administrative Expenses	1,805	
Total Marketing and Administrative Expenses		9,033
Operating Income		4,332
Interest Income	448	
Interest Expenses	550	
Total Other Income (Expenses)		(102)
Net Income Before Taxes		4,230
Income Taxes		1,438
Net Income		$2,792

Comparative Balance Sheets

	This Year-end	Last Year-end	Increase (Decrease)
Current Assets			
Cash	$1,983	$515	
Accounts Receivable	4,284	3,000	
Inventory	3,990	3,210	
Prepaid Insurance	60	180	
Total Current Assets	$10,317	$6,905	
Non-Current Assets			
Land	$2,000	$2,000	
Buildings and Equipment, net	7,904	10,068	
Investments - Long Term	5,600	3,200	
Total Non-Current Assets	$15,504	$15,268	
Total Assets	$25,821	$22,173	
Current Liabilities			
Accounts Payable	$632	$550	
Wages Payable	775	580	
Dividends Payable	400	400	
Taxes Payable	462	295	
Other Current Liabilities	492	380	
Total Current Liabilities	$2,761	$2,205	
Non-Current Liabilities			
Bonds Payable	$3,190	$1,090	
Long-term Debt	2,790	2,990	
Total Non-Current Liabilities	$5,980	$4,080	
Stockholders' Equity			
Common Stock, $1 par	$2,000	$2,000	
Capital in Excess of Par	8,110	8,110	
Retained Earnings	6,970	5,778	
Total Stockholders' Equity	$17,080	$15,888	
Total Liabilities + Stockholders' Equity	$25,821	$22,173	

Additional data from the General Ledger

	This Year
Depreciation expenses in 1992	$2,164
Purchase of Long Term Investment	2,400
Proceeds from the Sale of Bonds	2,100
Principle Payment of the Mortgage Payable	200
Dividends Paid	1,600

Worksheet 15   Like Magic Company

Statement of Cash Flows - For the Year End
Cash Flows from Operating Activities:
　Sales Revenue
　Changes in Accounts Receivable
　Cash Received from Customers
　Interest Income
　　Cash Provided by Operating Activities
　Cost of Goods Sold
　Marketing Expenses
　General and Administrative Expenses
　Less Depreciation
　Changes in Inventories
　Changes in Prepaid Insurance
　Changes in Accounts Payable
　Changes in Wages Payable
　Changes in Taxes Payable
　Changes in Other Current Liabilities
　Cash Payments to Suppliers and Employees
　Interest Paid
　Income Taxes Paid
　　Cash Disbursed for Operating Activities
Net Cash Provided by Operating Activities
Cash Flows from Investing Activities:
　Proceeds from Sale of Equipment
　Purchase of Property, Plant & Equipment
　Purchase of Long Term Investment
Net Cash Flow From Investing Activities
Cash Flows from Financing Activities:
　Proceeds from Sale of Bonds
　Proceeds from Sale of Stock
　Principle Payment of Long Term Debt
　Dividends Paid
Net Cash Flow From Financing Activities
Net Increase (Decrease) in Cash
Cash: last year-end
Cash: this year-end

Reconciliation of Net Income and Net Cash Flow from Operating Activity
　Net Income
　Adjustments to reconcile net income to net cash
　　provided by operating activities:
　Depreciation
　Changes in Accounts Receivable
　Changes in Inventories
　Changes in Prepaid Insurance
　Changes in Accounts Payable
　Changes in Wages Payable
　Changes in Taxes Payable
　Changes in Other Current Liabilities
　　Total Adjustments
Net Cash Provided by Operating Activities

LIKE MAGIC COMPANY

Chapter 16: Analysis of Financial Statements

A: Component Percentages and Year-to-Year Changes

A. LEARNING OBJECTIVES

1. Gain insight into the performance of a company through comparative analyses of their financial statements.
2. Learn to prepare a horizontal analysis showing dollar and percentage changes between two time periods.
3. Learn to prepare a common size form, or vertical analysis. This form relates a company's net income and expenses to their sales; and their assets, liabilities and equity to their total assets.
4. Use an electronic spreadsheet to build a model, which will prepare the comparative and common size analyses.

B. NARRATIVE

You have just returned from a meeting with Ruby Rockefeller, your friendly banker. The meeting was to arrange a line of credit with the bank that could be used for short-term borrowing. Ruby agreed that it was best to make the arrangement when Like Magic was in a good financial position and did not have an immediate need for the funds. You were thinking about Ruby's request. She not only asked for copies of your latest financial statements, but wanted to see a form comparing the statements for the last two years, showing both years in common size percentages. The bank wanted to see the trend in Like Magic's performance and to compare the company's statements with other similar firms.

You decided that Like Magic's management and stockholders would be interested in this information as a regular supplement to your financial statements. It seems most efficient to extend your electronic spreadsheet model to automatically produce a comparative form. The form should show:

1. The annual income statements and balance sheets for the last two years.

2. A horizontal analysis, showing the increase or decrease in each line item on both statements between the last two years in dollar amounts and percentages.

3. A vertical analysis, showing each income statement item as a component percentage of net sales for both years.

4. A vertical analysis, showing each balance sheet item as a component percentage of total assets for both years.

C. REQUIREMENTS

1. Review Worksheet 16, **Like Magic Company's Income Statements and Balance Sheets for the Years Ended December 31**. Note the information to be completed and how it will be calculated. Fill in a few rows of the Worksheet by hand.

2. Use Excel to open the file **COMPARE**.

3. Complete all of the columns in **Like Magic Company's Income Statements and Balance Sheets for the Years Ended December 31**.

   a. Enter formulas into the cells in column D to compute the increased or decreased dollar amounts from last year to this year for each line item.

   b. Enter formulas into the cells in column E to compute the increased or decreased percentage changes from last year to this year for each line item. Use last year as the base or denominator year.

   c. In columns F and G, enter formulas to calculate the component percentages for each Income Statement by calculating each line as a percentage of Sales. Format the data as percentages with two decimal places. (Hint: you might want to enter the cell location for Sales Revenue as an absolute row address rather than a relative address. This would allow you to use the copy command and speed up your completion of the entries.) (See D. Computer Information for Copying With Absolute Cell Addresses.)

   d. Enter formulas to calculate the component percentages for the Balance Sheet for both years by calculating each line as a percentage of Total Assets. Format the data as percentages with two decimal places. (Hint: again you might want to use copying with absolute cell addresses.)

4. Save your results in the file **COMPARER**.

5. Print the comparative statements. Before printing, insert your name in the Print Header Line. (See Print Header Line in Chapter 1.)

6. Interpret the financial statements. Are all the changes positive? Should Like Magic be worried by decreases in some of the items? Why is the percentage increase in sales so much greater than the percentage increase in net income? What information is revealed by the comparative component percentages? Should Like Magic be pleased or concerned about the changes between the years?

D. COMPUTER INFORMATION

1. Name of the file to be retrieved: **COMPARE**
2. Name of the file to save results: **COMPARER**
3. Cell locations for results: **D4-G47**

Copying With Absolute Or Relative Cell Addresses

Using the **Copy** command allows a user to become highly productive in creating accounting and financial spreadsheets. Frequently, we want to create a formula or relationship between two or more financial items to see the results, e.g., the change in sales between two years. The Copy command allows us to reproduce that formula or relationship across many financial items, e.g., the rest of the items in the income statement. We do this by entering the formula in one cell and using the Copy command to copy that formula to several other cells. The designers of the electronic spreadsheets knew that most of the time we wanted our copying to be relative. For example, in cell D5 we create the formula +B5 - C5, the difference between the sales in two years. Then we copied that formula from cell D5 to D6 to get the difference between the cost of goods sold in the two years. When Excel copied the formula it changed the rows in the new formula relative to where the results were being placed. The formula in cell D6 becomes +B6 - C6. Excel keeps track of the number of rows and columns between the cell location containing the formula and the cell locations of each cell element in the formula.

Sometimes when copying a formula we want to keep a cell location constant or absolute for one or more cell elements in the formula. This is what is required in creating the component percentages of each income statement item to sales revenue in the common size analysis, i.e., the sales figure in the denominator is kept constant. To keep a cell location absolute in a formula, we precede both the column and row portions of the cell location with a dollar sign, e.g., $B$5. For example, to put a formula for sales divided by sales for this year in cell F5 and keep the cell location of sales in the denominator absolute or constant, the formula should be B5/$B$5. Then, when that formula is copied, the numerator would change relative to the cell location of the result, but the denominator would always be cell B5, sales. If the above formula in F5 was copied to F6, the formula in cell F6 would be B6/$B$5.

Excel also allows you to indicate just the row portion or the column portion of a cell address as absolute in a formula. To do this, put the dollar sign either in front of the row or column portion, whichever should be kept absolute. Try creating a component percentage formula for sales for this year with only the row constant, and then copy the formula to the column for last year.

E. WORKSHEET 16: LIKE MAGIC COMPANY INCOME STATEMENTS and BALANCE SHEETS FOR THE YEARS ENDED DECEMBER 31.

F. CHECK FIGURES

	Percentage	Cell Location
Increase in Sales:	135.04%	E4
Net Income % of Sales for This Year:	7.94%	F14
Increase in Cash:	285.05%	E19
Total Current Assets % of Total Assets for This Year:	39.96%	F23

LIKE MAGIC COMPANY

Chapter 16: Analysis of Financial Statements

B: Ratio Analysis

(This ratio analysis can be completed without doing 16-A)

A. LEARNING OBJECTIVES

1. Gain insight into the profitability, liquidity and solvency of a company by using ratio analysis.
2. Learn to compute a number of widely used ratios in financial statement analysis and explain the significance of each.
3. Use an electronic spreadsheet to create graphs of the ratios for increased visual impact and comparisons.

B. NARRATIVE

Rodney Rukeyser and his investment group liked the financial statement analysis that you put together. After their review, they began talking about ratios as measures of the financial health of a company and the impact these ratios had on the price of the common stock. Rodney suggested that you use your electronic spreadsheet to calculate a number of ratios. Ronald Regan, one of the partners in the investment group, said that he liked pictures. He asked that the ratios be shown as graphs as well as in numerical form.

You decided to create a table including several ratios measuring profitability, liquidity and solvency. A bar and a line graph will be created to illustrate some of the ratios for your next meeting with Rodney, Ron and their group.

C. REQUIREMENTS

1. Review the Financial Ratio section at the bottom of Worksheet 16. Write the formula for the ratios in the Worksheet.

2. Retrieve the file **COMPARER** (or **COMPARE**, if you did not do Assignment 16-A).

3. The file contains a Table of Financial Ratios starting in row 55, and additional needed data that will be needed to compute the ratios.

4. Create formulas for all the ratios (or those specified by your instructor) for both years. Format all items in the table to two decimal places. Format the rate of return ratios and the dividend ratios as percentages.

a. To make your work more efficient, you might want to split the screen into two windows. Move the cell pointer to a row about three-quarters of the way down the screen. Select **Window** from the menu at the top of the screen, then select **Split** from the drop-down menu. In the bottom window show the cells where the ratios will be formulated and in the top window show the statement cells for the components of the ratios. With this window approach, you can see which cell locations are needed as you create the formulas for the ratios. Remove the split window when you have finished entering formulas to compute the ratios. To remove the split window, select **Window** from the menu at the top of the screen, then select **Remove Split** from the drop-down menu.

b. The data for many of the ratios will be taken from the income statement and the balance sheet. For some of the ratios you will need the **Additional Year-end Data** and/or the **Relevant Data - Year Prior to Last Year** given in the rows above the financial ratios.

5. Save your results in the file **COMPARER.**

6. Print the Table of Financial Ratios.

7. Create, save and print the following graphs: (See the Appendix on Graphing Data to See Relationships, for computer information on graphing.)

   a. A bar graph showing the Current Ratio, Quick Ratio, and Inventory Turnover for both years.

   b. A line graph showing the Return on Sales, Return on Common Equity, and Return on Total Assets for both years.

8. Analyze and comment on Like Magic's performance using the ratios you developed.

D. COMPUTER INFORMATION

1. Name of the file to be retrieved: **COMPARER**
2. Name of the file to save results: **COMPARER**
4. Cell location for results: **B55-C69**

E. WORKSHEET 16: Table of Financial Ratios

F. CHECK FIGURES

	Ratio	Cell Location
Current Ratio This Year:	3.74	B55
Total Debt to Equity This Year	.51	B61
Earnings per Share, Common Last Year:	.77	C65

Worksheet 16 — Like Magic Company

Like Magic Company — Income Statements: Years Ended December 31

	This Year	Last Year	Increase (Decrease) Amount	Percent	Percentages of Sales This Year	Last Year
Sales revenue	$35,185	$14,970				
Cost of goods sold	21,820	8,950				
Gross profit	13,365	6,020				
Marketing expenses	7,228	2,930				
General and administrative expenses	1,805	670				
Operating income	4,332	2,420				
Interest income	448	400				
Interest expenses	550	250				
Net income before taxes	4,230	2,570				
Income taxes	1,438	1,028				
Net income	$2,792	$1,542				

Like Magic Company — Balance Sheets: Years Ended December 31

	This Year	Last Year	Increase (Decrease) Amount	Percent	Percentages of Assets This Year	Last Year
Current assets						
Cash	$1,983	$515				
Accounts receivable	4,284	3,000				
Inventory	3,990	3,210				
Prepaid insurance	60	180				
Total current assets	$10,317	$6,905				
Non-current assets						
Land	$2,000	$2,000				
Buildings & equipment, net	7,904	10,068				
Investments - long term	5,600	3,200				
Total non-current assets	$15,504	$15,268				
Total assets	$25,821	$22,173				
Current liabilities						
Accounts payable	$632	$550				
Wages payable	775	580				
Dividends payable	400	400				
Taxes payable	462	295				
Other current liabilities	492	380				
Total current liabilities	$2,761	$2,205				
Non-current liabilities						
Bonds payable	$3,190	$1,090				
Long-term debt	2,790	2,990				
Total non-current liabilities	$5,980	$4,080				
Stockholders' equity						
Common stock, $1 par	$2,000	$2,000				
Capital in excess of par	8,110	8,110				
Retained earnings	6,970	5,778				
Total stockholders' equity	$17,080	$15,888				
Liabilities + stockholder's equity	$25,821	$22,173				

Worksheet 16 Like Magic Company

Additional Year-end Data	This Year	Last Year	Relevant Data - Year Prior to Last Year	
Closing market price	25	17	Inventory	$1,524
Dividends	1600	800	Accounts receivable	2,388
Shares of common stock outstanding	2000	2000	Stockholders' equity	11,634
			Total assets	14,183

Financial Ratios	This Year	Last Year
Current ratio		
Quick ratio		
Inventory turnover		
Accounts receivable turnover		
Collection period - days		
Current debt to equity		
Total debt to equity		
Return on sales		
Return on common equity		
Return on total assets		
Earnings per share, common		
Price-earnings ratio		
Dividend yield, common		
Dividend payout		
Book value per share, common		

LIKE MAGIC COMPANY

Appendix

Excel – Enhancing Your Skills

This appendix is included to help you complete the assignments in this book. It is directed at improving your productivity when using Excel. The topics are to teach or remind you about certain key skills. This appendix is not a guide for beginning to learn Excel, nor is it a complete reference on Excel. Use the *Help* command in Excel to get answers to your questions.

The word **Select** is used throughout this book to indicate action that you the user must take to make Excel do the tasks you want done. When the text says **Select**, use the mouse to move the pointer to the appropriate cell(s), command or arrow and press the left mouse key. If a group of cells are indicated, move the pointer to the first cell, press and hold the left mouse key, drag the pointer to the last cell indicated, and release the left mouse key.

1. Main Menu

The main menu in Excel is composed of commands shown across the top of the screen such as: **file, edit, help**, etc. Selecting any of these commands will show a list of lower level commands. Selecting one of these lower level commands will in turn provide additional commands or choices that need to be made to complete the task. The following are brief discussions of some of the commands that will be used to complete the assignments.

File, Open – Open is a command under File to bring information from a disk into active memory and onto the screen. The file must be active so the information can be viewed and additional entries or changes made. Selecting Open produces a drop-down menu used to select the: file name, directory on the hard disk drive, disk drives (A, floppy or C, hard disk), and file type (Excel workbook, Lotus 1-2-3, etc.). To begin each assignment you must select File, select Open, use the down arrow to select floppy disk drive A, select the file name (CVP for Chapter 2), and select OK.

File, Save and **Save As** – Save and Save As are commands under File. These are used to take information from the screen and active memory and make a copy onto a disk. The menus and selections are similar to Open.

File, Print and **Page Setup** – Print and Page Setup are commands under File to control printing. Page Setup can be used to change margins, enter Headers and Footers, etc. (See Print Header Line in Chapter 1 for entering your name in a header.)

Edit, Copy and **Paste** – Copy and Paste are commands under Edit. They are used to take data or a formula that is in one cell and reproduce it in a second cell while leaving the original in the first cell. You can copy data or a formula from one cell and paste it into one or several cells. You can copy from several cells with one copy command. The cell or cells copied from must be selected first, before the Copy command is selected. Similarly, the cell or cells copied to must be pointed to before selecting the Paste command. If you have a formula in a cell, you can copy just the numerical results (not the formula) to a second cell by selecting **Paste Special**, then selecting **Values**. (The section below on Copying Data Containing Cell References should be read to enhance your ability to use Excel.)

Insert – The insert command is used to insert rows, columns, charts, etc. into the spreadsheet. (See Chart later in the appendix for a discussion on creating a chart or graph.)

Format, Cells – Cells is a command under Format. It is used to display a cell(s) as a number, percentage, date, etc.; and to specify dollar signs, commas, number of decimal places, etc.

Tools, Data Analysis – Data Analysis is a command under Tools. It is used to have Excel perform statistical analyses such as regression.

Window, Split and **Freeze Panes** – Split and Freeze Panes are commands under Window. Both are used to separate the window or viewing area on the screen into different sections. This is useful when you want different parts of the spreadsheet, which are many rows or columns apart, to be visible on the screen at the same time. For example: if rows 1-23 are visible on the screen, select row 11 along the left side of the screen, select Windows, select Freeze Panes, then scrolling down the rows using the down arrow on the right would keep the top rows, 1-10, visible on the screen. To end the separate windows, select Window, and select **Unfreeze Panes**.

Help – Help is a command to get information on using Excel.

2. Entering Data and Formulas

Formulas with Cell References vs. Numerical Entries – Enter formulas with cell references and let Excel do the computation whenever possible. Doing this will save time and effort since many assignments in this book require changing the starting data or running "what if" analyses. A formula should be used even when numerical data in one cell is to be inserted into a second cell. For example, if $8500 is the figure for sales in cell B3 and should also be shown as part of an income statement in cell B18, then in cell B18 enter the formula =**B3**, and Excel will copy $8500 from B3 to B18. If you later adjust the sales figure in cell B3, Excel will automatically adjust every successive figure that is related to it through a formula. Also, Chapter 2-B, requirement 2, requires calculating the contribution margin per unit and ratios for six sets of data. If you enter formulas with cell references to compute those two results for one set of data, then copy those formulas to each of the other five columns, Excel will calculate the results for the entire six columns. If you computed the results by hand and then keyed the numeric data in, you would have to repeat the hand computation and keying six different times.

Error, ##### - If a ##### is displayed in a cell it indicates that the numeric result of a formula is too long. You can widen the cell length, decrease the number of decimal places or make other changes so the numerical result is displayed on the screen.

Error, #N/A, #DIV/0, #NUM!, #REF!, #VALUE! – are examples of error terms that Excel may display in a cell. They indicate that the formula contains an error value or reference.

3. Copying Data Containing Cell References

Relative Cell References – When a formula is copied from one cell to another, Excel keeps track of the number of rows and columns between the cells and adjusts any cell references in the formulas by an equal number of rows and columns. Chapter 2-B, requirement 3, requires calculating the total fixed expenses for six sets of fixed expenses in columns C-H. The first total fixed expense will go into cell **C42**, as a formula **+C39+C40+C41**. Thus the total fixed expense in cell C42 will equal the sum of the fixed expenses given in the three cells directly above cell C42. If we now copy this formula for the total fixed expense for the first set of data, column C, to the other five columns, Excel will compute the total of fixed expenses in each column. Excel will make relative adjustments to the cell references as follows: Column D holds the second set of fixed expenses and the total fixed expenses shown in cell **D42,** will be the formula **+D39+D40+D41**. Column E holds the third set of fixed expenses and the total fixed expenses shown in cell **E42,** will be the formula **+E39+E40+E41**. Column F holds the fourth set of fixed expenses and the total fixed expenses shown in cell **F42,** will be the formula **+F39+F40+F41** And so on. Thus Excel has adjusted each formula for the total fixed expenses making each relative to the cells in the same column above it.

Absolute Cell References – Sometimes when a formula is copied from one cell to another, we don't want some or all the cell references in the formula to change relative to the cell receiving the formula. In this case, we want to keep a cell reference location exactly the same, or **absolute**, no matter the cell location where we paste the formula. A cell reference is made **absolute** by putting $ in front of both the row number and column letter, e.g. $A$1. Chapter 2-A, requirement 7, requires the calculation of sales dollars for a single selling price and nine different figures of units sold. The sales dollars in each of nine successive cells, B23-J23, will be the single selling price, C4, times the units sold figure in the cells right above the sales dollars, B22-J22. To increase efficiency, we create a formula in the cell for the first sales dollars that keeps the cell reference to the selling price absolute, **$C$4**. To compute the first sales dollars in cell **B23**, we create the formula **$C$4*B22**. Then we copy that formula to the cells for the other sales dollars, C23-J23. Now, the second sales dollars figure shown in cell **C23**, will be the formula **$C$4*C22**. The third sales dollars figure shown in cell **D23**, will be the formula **$C$4*D22**. The fourth sales dollars figure shown in cell **E23**, will be the formula **$C$4*E22**. And so on. Excel will hold the cell reference for the sales price absolute, **$C$4,** and change the cell references for the units sold, **B22-J22**, relative to the location of the cells for the sales dollars, C23-J23.

Mixed Cell Reference – Sometimes only a row number or column letter should be made absolute in a cell reference. (See Absolute Cell Reference above.) Putting a $ just in front of the row number or column letter will keep only that part of the cell reference absolute. Try it to see how it works.

4. Charts and Graphs

Chart is the term used in Excel for a graph. A chart can either be *embedded* on a worksheet, so it is displayed near the associated data for the chart, or it can placed on a separate sheet that accompanies the sheet containing the data. Embedded charts are viewed on the screen and printed on the same page as the data used for the chart. If a chart is placed on a separate sheet, the chart and the data cannot be viewed on the screen at the same time, and they are printed on two separate pages.

Before a Chart is Created – Give serious thought to which data will be used for a chart and where the data should be located in the spreadsheet. Creating a chart is easier and the display will be more effective if the associated data is arranged in cells with the chart in mind. It is helpful to orient the data to be charted in consecutive rows or columns of the same number of cells for line and bar charts. One or two word descriptions placed as headers in an adjacent row or column can be easily used to add clarity and information to the chart.

Data to Chart – Use the mouse to select, point to and highlight the cells containing the data to chart.

Chart Wizard – Using the Chart Wizard in Excel will simplify the creation of the chart. Begin the Wizard be selecting **Insert**, then select the **icon with the vertical bars** from the drop-down menu, or directly select the icon with the vertical bars if it is visible on the menu at the top of the screen. The Chart Wizard uses the following four steps to create a chart. (You might want to review the discussion in Chapter 3-A, requirement 6, for an example of creating and modifying a chart.)

Chart Type – The chart type is selected in step one from several types of bar, line, XY, pie and other charts. There are several variations for each type. For instance, on line and XY charts the data points can be plotted with or without lines connecting them.

Chart Source Data – If the sample chart looks good, select **Next**. If not, you can select **Series** and enter cell ranges to be plotted, or you can select **Cancel**, and select new data to chart.

Chart Options – Step three is Chart Options, which can be used to enter titles, labels, place the legend, etc.

Chart Location – Chart Location is used to place the chart as either an embedded object on the data sheet, or as a separate sheet. An embedded chart can be resized and/or moved around the spreadsheet as follows: First, click in the chart area so the black boxes appear on the borders. Next, move the pointer to a side or corner of the chart so the pointer changes to a double-headed arrow. Then click and drag the side or corner to resize or move the chart. Finally, click outside of the chart.

Changing a Chart – A chart can be changed either before or after it is created. Before finishing, either select **Back** at any step of the Chart Wizard to return to the previous step, or select **Cancel** to delete what you have done. If the chart is finished, select it so it is active on the screen. If the chart is in a separate sheet, select the chart name from the menu at the bottom of the screen. If it is embedded, select it by clicking anywhere in the chart area. When the chart is active, select the Chart Wizard to change it.

Deleting a Chart – Make the chart active. If the chart is in a separate sheet, select the chart name from the menu at the bottom of the screen. If it is embedded, select it by clicking anywhere in the chart area. When the chart is active, press the **Delete** key.

DATA DISK LICENSE AGREEMENT AND LIMITED WARRANTY

READ THIS LICENSE CAREFULLY BEFORE OPENING THE DISKETTE PACKAGE. BY OPENING THIS PACKAGE, YOU ARE AGREEING TO THE TERMS AND CONDITIONS OF THIS LICENSE. IF YOU DO NOT AGREE, DO NOT OPEN THE PACKAGE. PROMPTLY RETURN THE UNOPENED PACKAGE AND ALL ACCOMPANYING ITEMS TO THE PLACE YOU OBTAINED THEM. THESE TERMS APPLY TO ALL LICENSED SOFTWARE ON THE DISK EXCEPT THAT THE TERMS FOR USE OF ANY SHAREWARE OR FREEWARE ON THE DISKETTES ARE AS SET FORTH IN THE ELECTRONIC LICENSE LOCATED ON THE DISK:

1. **GRANT OF LICENSE and OWNERSHIP:** The enclosed data disk ("Software") is licensed, not sold, to you by Prentice-Hall, Inc. ("We" or the "Company") for academic purposes and in consideration of your purchase or adoption of the accompanying Company textbooks and/or other materials, and your agreement to these terms. This license allows instructors and students enrolled in the course using the Company textbook that accompanies this Software (the "Course") to use, display and manipulate the data for academic use only, so long as you comply with the terms of this Agreement. We reserve any rights not granted to you. You own only the disk(s) but we and our licensors own the Software itself.

2. **RESTRICTIONS ON USE AND TRANSFER:** You may not transfer, distribute or make available the Software or the Documentation, except to instructors and students in your school in connection with the Course. You may not reverse engineer, disassemble, decompile, modify, adapt, translate or create derivative works based on the Software or the Documentation. You may be held legally responsible for any copying or copyright infringement which is caused by your failure to abide by the terms of these restrictions.

3. **TERMINATION:** This license is effective until terminated. This license will terminate automatically without notice from the Company if you fail to comply with any provisions or limitations of this license. Upon termination, you shall destroy the Documentation and all copies of the Software. All provisions of this Agreement as to limitation and disclaimer of warranties, limitation of liability, remedies or damages, and our ownership rights shall survive termination.

4. **DISCLAIMER OF WARRANTY: THE COMPANY AND ITS LICENSORS MAKE NO WARRANTIES ABOUT THE SOFTWARE, WHICH IS PROVIDED "AS-IS." IF THE DISK IS DEFECTIVE IN MATERIALS OR WORKMANSHIP, YOUR ONLY REMEDY IS TO RETURN IT TO THE COMPANY WITHIN 30 DAYS FOR REPLACEMENT UNLESS THE COMPANY DETERMINES IN GOOD FAITH THAT THE DISK HAS BEEN MISUSED OR IMPROPERLY INSTALLED, REPAIRED, ALTERED OR DAMAGED. THE COMPANY DISCLAIMS ALL WARRANTIES, EXPRESS OR IMPLIED, INCLUDING WITHOUT LIMITATION, THE IMPLIED WARRANTIES OF MERCHANTABILITY AND FITNESS FOR A PARTICULAR PURPOSE. THE COMPANY DOES NOT WARRANT, GUARANTEE OR MAKE ANY REPRESENTATION REGARDING THE ACCURACY, RELIABILITY, CURRENTNESS, USE, OR RESULTS OF USE, OF THE SOFTWARE.**

5. **LIMITATION OF REMEDIES AND DAMAGES: IN NO EVENT, SHALL THE COMPANY OR ITS EMPLOYEES, AGENTS, LICENSORS OR CONTRACTORS BE LIABLE FOR ANY INCIDENTAL, INDIRECT, SPECIAL OR CONSEQUENTIAL DAMAGES ARISING OUT OF OR IN CONNECTION WITH THIS LICENSE OR THE SOFTWARE, INCLUDING, WITHOUT LIMITATION, LOSS OF USE, LOSS OF DATA, LOSS OF INCOME OR PROFIT, OR OTHER LOSSES SUSTAINED AS A RESULT OF INJURY TO ANY PERSON, OR LOSS OF OR DAMAGE TO PROPERTY, OR CLAIMS OF THIRD PARTIES, EVEN IF THE COMPANY OR AN AUTHORIZED REPRESENTATIVE OF THE COMPANY HAS BEEN ADVISED OF THE POSSIBILITY OF SUCH DAMAGES. SOME JURISDICTIONS DO NOT ALLOW THE LIMITATION OF DAMAGES IN CERTAIN CIRCUMSTANCES, SO THE ABOVE LIMITATIONS MAY NOT ALWAYS APPLY.**

6. **GENERAL:** THIS AGREEMENT SHALL BE CONSTRUED IN ACCORDANCE WITH THE LAWS OF THE UNITED STATES OF AMERICA AND THE STATE OF NEW YORK, APPLICABLE TO CONTRACTS MADE IN NEW YORK, AND SHALL BENEFIT THE COMPANY, ITS AFFILIATES AND ASSIGNEES. This Agreement is the complete and exclusive statement of the agreement between you and the Company and supersedes all proposals, prior agreements, oral or written, and any other communications between you and the company or any of its representatives relating to the subject matter. If you are a U.S. Government user, this Software is licensed with "restricted rights" as set forth in subparagraphs (a)-(d) of the Commercial Computer-Restricted Rights clause at FAR 52.227-19 or in subparagraphs (c)(1)(ii) of the Rights in Technical Data and Computer Software clause at DFARS 252.227-7013, and similar clauses, as applicable.

Should you have any questions concerning this agreement or if you wish to contact the Company for any reason, please contact in writing:

> Director of New Media
> Higher Education Division
> Prentice Hall, Inc.
> 1 Lake Street
> Upper Saddle River, NJ 07458